MARK WITAS

REVIEW AND HERALD®
PUBLISHING ASSOCIATION
Since 1861 | www.reviewandherald.com

To order additional copies of *Living Out Loud,* by Mark Witas,
call 1-800-765-6955.

Visit us at **www.reviewandherald.com** for information on other
Review and Herald® products.

———————

Copyright © 2011 by Review and Herald® Publishing Association

Published by Review and Herald® Publishing Association, Hagerstown, MD 21741-1119

Review and Herald® titles may be purchased in bulk for educational, business, fund-raising, or sales promotional use. For information, e-mail SpecialMarkets@reviewandherald.com.

The Review and Herald® Publishing Association publishes biblically based materials for spiritual, physical, and mental growth and Christian discipleship.

The author assumes full responsibility for the accuracy of all facts and quotations as cited in this book.

Unless otherwise noted, Bible texts in this book are from the *Holy Bible, New International Version.* Copyright © 1973, 1978, 1984, International Bible Society. Used by permission of Zondervan Bible Publishers.

Bible texts credited to NKJV are from the New King James Version. Copyright © 1979, 1980, 1982 by Thomas Nelson, Inc. Used by permission. All rights reserved.

Bible texts credited to NRSV are from the New Revised Standard Version of the Bible, copyright © 1989 by the Division of Christian Education of the National Council of the Churches of Christ in the U.S.A. Used by permission.

Bible texts credited to TNIV are from the *Holy Bible, Today's New International Version.* Copyright © 2001, 2005 by International Bible Society. Used by permission of International Bible Society. All rights reserved worldwide.

This book was
Edited by Kalie Kelch
Copyedited by Judy Blodgett
Cover designed by Ron Pride
Cover art by Thinkstock.com
Typeset: Minion 10.5/14

PRINTED IN U.S.A.
15 14 13 12 11   5 4 3 2 1

Library of Congress Cataloging-in-Publication Data
Witas, Mark, 1962-   .
  Living out loud / Mark Witas.
      p. cm.
  1. Christian life—Anecdotes. 2. Conduct of life—Anecdotes. I. Title.
  BV4517.W58 2011
  248.4—dc22

                    2010044072

ISBN 979-0-8280-2450-1

CONTENTS

NEW

"Therefore, if anyone is in Christ, he is a new creation;
the old has gone, the new has come!"
2 Corinthians 5:17.

Not everyone likes new things or ways of doing things—change can be hard. In fact, most of us like things to stay the same. It's a comfort thing.

As we were growing up, my sister and I did a lot of weird things. (Mostly, she was the one who was strange, but don't tell her I said that!) One of the things about her that I thought was kind of weird was that she had a blankie. Somewhere early on, my sister got attached to a blue blanket that she (and the whole family) lovingly referred to as "blankie."

Blankie was a vital part of my sister's existence. We couldn't go anywhere as a family without blankie. If we were to accidentally leave blankie at home, we'd have to turn around and get it before we could complete the rest of our trip. My sister couldn't sleep without blankie. She brought blankie to the table for every meal. Blankie was drenched with love—and dirt and food and pet hair.

By the time my sister was 10 years old, blankie was less of a blanket and more of a remnant of memories. Blankie was a dirty rag. Dozens of times my dad and mom tried to convince my sister that it was time to take blankie to the blankie cemetery and say goodbye. But each time my sister wailed, wept, and clung to blankie like a mother would her baby. It was obvious that blankie wasn't going anywhere.

Finally, thinking that if she didn't do something soon blankie would be so dirty that it would take on a life of its own, Mom tried one more plan. She asked my grandma to make a new blanket very similar in looks and feel to blankie, only cleaner and less horrible.

One night, when my sister was asleep, Mom switched the new blanket with blankie. The next morning we all woke up to what I thought was a siren. It was my sister. When she discovered that blankie was gone, she screamed a scream that can only come from a person who has lost their true love. She got blankie back. And to my knowledge, she still has a part of that remnant of a rag hidden somewhere among her most cherished things.

Jesus says that He wants to take our old life and give us a new one. He wants us to be a new creation. But for some reason a lot of people have grown so attached to the way they do things that they choose not to give everything to Jesus. They are afraid that if they give Jesus everything, He'll take something away that they really want or like.

Of course, nothing could be further from the truth. Jesus says that when we take the leap of faith and let Him make "all things new" He will exchange our old life for a new life of abundant living! And that's a goal of every Christian—to live a more abundant life!

God, please make me new in You every day. Help me to let You work freely in my life, without any hesitation or fear of change, knowing that You have my best interest at heart. Help me to grow in love, in grace, and in Your mercy so that I may become more like You each day. Amen.

ANOTHER CHANCE

"To him who overcomes, I will give the right to eat from the tree of life,
which is in the paradise of God."
Revelation 2:7.

One of the challenges that Wendy and I faced after we got married was the reality that we don't have a lot in common. I'm tall; she's . . . not tall. I'm a typical sanguine life of the party; Wendy likes to sit in the corner and read a book. She likes dogs; I like cats. I like to play team and individual sports; she likes to watch ice skating. She's talented and beautiful and, well, you get the picture.

We had been married less than a year when Wendy decided that she needed to remedy the situation. She figured that we needed something in common that we could share recreationally. So, taking matters into her own hands, she went out and bought me a present for my twenty-fifth birthday. She bought me ice skates.

Growing up in western Canada gave Wendy the opportunity to learn how to skate quite well. In fact, by the time she was in college, she joined a team that did choreographed ice dancing. She could spin and jump and land in graceful manners only imagined by somebody as tall and uncoordinated as I.

When I unwrapped the skates, I didn't know what to say. Not only had I never wanted ice skates, I'd never even been to an ice rink. I had always figured that if God wanted me to walk on ice, He'd have made me a polar bear.

I tried to look enthusiastic and grateful for my gift. Wendy excitedly explained that now we'd have something to do together. She had romantic images dancing in her head of Olympic ice-skating couples wearing sequin body tights, gliding across the ice in each other's arms.

My sister, niece, and wife convinced me that I'd be a great skater, and they made a date for all of us to go skating the next Saturday night at the local rink. As the day approached, I actually became anxious to conquer the very real fear I had of wearing sharp blades on my feet and sliding around with them on a slippery surface.

The night came, and we went to the ice rink. I sat on the bleachers and laced up my skates for the first time. I'm already six feet six inches tall. Throw skates on my feet and I'm an NBA player with dangerous weapons on my feet!

My wife, sister, and 5-year-old niece were already out on the rink, gliding along with the greatest of ease, when I slipped onto the ice. Balance was my first problem, so I grabbed the side boards and inched my way along the side of the rink, being as cautious as I could. Soon I gained the confidence to push myself from one side board to another. Everything seemed to be going great, as long as I didn't try to turn or stop. I could actually get enough momentum going so that I looked like I was kind of ice skating, so I decided to take the risk and venture out into the middle of the rink with all the rest of the Michelle Kwan wannabes.

I lined myself up in the direction of the middle of the rink and gave myself a shove. With arms flailing, legs shaking, and courage high, I ventured from the safety of the side boards to the middle of the rink. Mind you, I looked like a novice with severe body control challenges, but hey, I had to start somewhere.

As I gained momentum and joined the flow of the ice-skating crowd, I looked up from my unstable feet and saw what—up to that point—was the scariest thing I'd ever seen. Coming toward me at an alarming rate of speed was a woman nearly my size. I don't know her name, but for the sake of the story, let's call her Helga.

I yelled, "You're going the wrong way!"

Helga yelled back, "I know!"

I yelled, "I can't turn!"

Helga yelled back, "I can't either!"

People who teach physics like to ask the question "What happens when an immovable object meets an irresistible force?" I've never taken physics, but I know the answer. Helga and I collided in the middle of that ice rink. I think Helga was the immovable object, because she sent me flying swiftly backward. I landed so hard on my tailbone that I thought my spine was jutting through the top of my head. I'd never felt so much pain. Women who have gone through natural childbirth have not felt the pain I felt that night—I can guarantee it (although some might argue with me on this point). And that was just the physical pain.

The emotional pain happened when I looked up to see my "ice dancing partner" teetering like a tall tree in the wind. I started to pray like the psalm-ist, "Please, God, send a mighty wind and blow my foe the other way."

He didn't. She fell right on top of me, pinning me to the ice; her face smashed against mine. My request was simple and to the point: "Please get off me."

She did. I crawled to the edge of the rink, gingerly climbed over the boards, and walked back to the grandstands where some people sat and watched the skaters. I took my birthday skates off, found a young man with feet about my size, and gave them to him.

So ended my dreams of being a star for the Vancouver Canucks. I had a bad experience, and I threw in the towel. The going got tough, and the tough gave his ice skates away. I've never skated since.

It may be that you have had a bad experience that has soured your view of God or the church. Don't do what I did with my ice skates. Don't give up! God needs you. Life on this earth is a marathon filled with plenty of ups and downs to discourage you. But keep your eye on the prize! And remember, God—your trainer, coach, cheerleader, and running partner—is right there beside you. Don't let anything or anyone steal your crown.

Dear Jesus, give me strength to run the race of life. Help me to be faithful to the end. Help me to keep my eyes on the prize so that I may never give up my pursuit of You and the life You want me to live. Amen.

TOSS THOSE COOKIES

"Do not take revenge, my friends, but leave room for God's wrath, for it is written: 'It is mine to avenge; I will repay,' says the Lord."
Romans 12:19.

Poetic justice has a way of making people grin. There is nothing like the feeling of seeing someone get what they deserve, especially if that someone has wronged you on more than one occasion.

Let me give you an example. There was a rivalry that had developed between the boys' and girls' dormitories at Bella Coola Adventist Academy. It all started one day when some of the girls in the dorm had picked blackberries and spent all afternoon baking cobbler. When they took the mouthwatering dessert out of the oven, they placed the dish on the windowsill to cool.

It wasn't long before the smell of the bubbling, gooey delight wafted its way to the porch at the boys' dorm across the yard. When that tempting fragrance floated into the nostrils of a few of the boys hanging out on the stairs, well, let's just say that cobbler came to a quick end. The only thing left of the cobbler was a crumb or two on the cheeks of the cobbler thieves and an empty dish on the windowsill of the girls' dorm.

Less than 10 minutes later an angry girls' dean and three upset bakers pounded on my apartment door. They were upset, and rightfully so. You see, it wasn't the first time the boys had sneaked over and brought a tasty dish to an untimely end. The girls wanted justice, and they wanted it now. Of course, when I asked the boys who the guilty party was, nobody confessed, which made the girls even angrier. That's when I saw Penny get a little grin on her face and walk back to the dorm. I had no idea what she was up to, but knowing Penny, somehow revenge was about to happen.

A few days later some of the girls let it be known that they were baking cookies that afternoon. And they made it known that they were not in the mood for any shenanigans. The boys were to leave their cookies alone.

Of course, that afternoon when they set the cookies on the windowsill to cool, some of the boys (like ninjas) sneaked the cookies back to their dorm rooms and had a feast. About an hour later Penny asked if she could come over to the dorm and make an announcement after worship.

After worship that evening, Penny came in and addressed the boys. "We thought we made it clear that you guys were to stay away from our cookies today." A few snickers could be heard from some of the suspects sitting in the room.

"But we knew that we were dealing with boys, and boys are too immature to have any kind of self-control." More snickering.

"So we decided that if you weren't going to learn your lesson the easy way, we would teach you a lesson the hard way." Now my curiosity was roused. What did they do?

Penny had a bowl with her that was covered by a cloth. She said, "I thought you'd like to know the ingredients we used to bake the cookies today." Penny uncovered the bowl and pointed at what looked like little chocolate candies. But they weren't candies.

Penny dropped the bombshell. "This is deer poop. This is the special ingredient we put in the cookies today. This is the special ingredient that some of you have in your digestive system right now."

She continued, "From now on you will never know what is in the things we bake, so the choice is yours—wait until supper and eat the dessert we make, or steal it ahead of time and take your chances. Oh, and when we were in the woods gleaning the deer poop, we found lots of other interesting stuff to add whenever we suspect you can't control yourselves again."

With that, she smiled, curtsied, and left.

For a moment there was silence. Then four boys flew out of the room with a sick look on their faces.

I don't remember if Penny got in trouble for what she did, but I do know that the boys didn't steal anything from the windowsill of the girls' dorm kitchen anymore.

This was a childish prank, but all too often people feel as though they have to take situations into their own hands and exact revenge—even though Jesus asks the complete opposite of His followers. Jesus would rather have us forgive and gain a friend than exact revenge and gain an enemy. More Christians need to listen to the Lord when He says, "Vengeance is Mine."

Jesus, help me always to remember that You are my defender. No matter how hard it is, help me to leave revenge at the foot of the cross. Amen.

ROCKS

*"Come to me, all you who are weary and burdened,
and I will give you rest."*
Matthew 11:28.

Iused to teach at a school in the middle of nowhere in British Columbia, Canada, that took all its students and teachers backpacking once a month. In truth, one of the reasons we had the program was that our gymnasium was big enough only to play a game of *Twister* in—if you folded the game mat in half.

I always looked forward to the first backpacking trip of the new school year. Each year we'd get a lot of kids who were the "outdoors" type. We would also get a small group who would come to the school from big cities—kids who had only heard about trees and thought that milk came from cartons and not cows.

Cora was one of those kids. Her biggest concern during the trip was that she'd inadvertently break a fingernail. Cora was a nice girl who had a special gift. I wouldn't call it a spiritual gift, but she was good at it. Cora had the gift of whining in a tone of voice that could break glass. The sound of fingernails running down a blackboard was more pleasant than the sound of Cora whining. And Cora decided that she was going to use her gift to the fullest on our first backpacking trip.

The trip was split up between days of backpacking and canoeing. In all, we'd pack about 30 miles and canoe five lakes. When Cora heard this, she started in: "Why do we have to do this? Why can't I stay home? Why is my pack so heavy? Why doesn't anyone want to hike with me?" Finally I told her that if she'd be quiet, the grizzly bears wouldn't hear her. She whined a little less.

On this particular trip it was my job to bring up the rear of the group. Usually I didn't mind this job, but this time was different. I had to walk behind Cora. The first day was only three miles of up-and-down hiking. Nothing big. Cora made the trip seem like 15 miles. I knew the next day was really going to try my patience. It was a 10-mile hike, nearly seven miles was uphill, with no water on the trail. The question wasn't if Cora could make the hike; it was whether she could make the hike without my putting a large piece of duct tape over her mouth. I knew that somehow I had to amuse myself or I would go crazy, so I thought of a plan.

As we packed up the hill, every time Cora whined I'd secretly slip a rock in the loose parts of her backpack. The more she whined, the more rocks I slipped in. All the way up the hill she whined. All the way up the hill I giggled. For some reason I got joy out of seeing the sweat, the faces, and hearing the verbal agony coming from Cora as she unknowingly carried more and more rocks up the mountain.

Finally we reached Turner Lake, the destination for the day's hike. She took off her pack and started looking through the pockets for a spare candy bar to give her a needed boost of energy. As she started to discover the quarry of rocks in her pack, she did what I didn't expect—she started to laugh. She looked up at me and said, "You did this, didn't you!"

"Yep! And if you keep whining, I'll do more!" She stopped whining. She actually seemed to have a genuinely good time the rest of the trip.

Without knowing it, Cora's burden got heavier and heavier. She was carrying needless weight up the mountain. She was struggling harder than she needed to struggle.

Wow! What a life lesson. I know hundreds of people just like Cora. They travel up the mountain of life with rocks in their backpack, and they don't even know it. Weighing them down are such things as grudges, sins that aren't forgiven, or bad habits.

The funny thing is that they don't need to have the weight of this stuff in their lives. Jesus' open invitation is "Come to Me, and I will give you rest!" What an offer! What a God!

Dear Jesus, please help me to rest in You. Keep the weight of the world off my back. Help me to daily breathe in You and let You carry my burdens. Thank You for Your unfailing love and guidance. Amen.

WAVES

I think the reason I like Peter more than all the other disciples is because, like me, much of the time he would act and then think. I don't recommend that kind of action. In fact, it's gotten me into all kinds of trouble. More than once I've committed to an action that, in retrospect, I wish I would have thought about first.

I think the time that still gives me goose bumps was what I like to call "the closest I've ever come to death." I was hiking up the side of a mountain with some of my students when I noticed on one side of the trail a rock wall that probably stood 70 feet from the base. It looked very climbable from the bottom. I asked the guys if any of them wanted to climb it with me. They all politely (and wisely) declined. I said, "OK, chicken livers, meet me on the top of the wall." They zipped up the trail to meet me on top, and I started to climb.

At first the climb was easy. There were lots of knobs and crags to grab and pull myself up. I was having a great time. My goal was to climb the wall and reach the top before my students could hike there. Everything was going according to plan until I reached a point on the wall where it didn't seem as though I was going to be able to go any farther. I wasn't (and am still not) an experienced climber. I had no ropes. I just had my spirit of adventure and a seemingly small brain. I was 50 feet in the air with nowhere to go.

I looked down to see what would happen if I just dropped. From my vantage point bad things would happen if I fell. I looked up for the next handhold or a place to put my foot, but I couldn't see or feel anything to advance up the rock. I was stuck.

Pretty soon I noticed that my grip was starting to loosen. I was getting weak. I was starting to lose hope until some of my students looked over the edge and said, "We chicken livers seem to be in a better place than you are right now!"

"I'm stuck. Can you guys see anything for me to grab on to up there?"

They looked down the wall and finally said, "Yes, but you will have to lunge at it to get it." They described a great hold for me that was just out of my sight to my right.

I had to make a decision. *Do I trust my students and lunge for what I cannot see? Or do I fall anyway?* I decided to trust and lunge. I did. It worked, and I climbed up the rest of the way.

I'm pretty sure Peter had similar feelings as Jesus beckoned him to get out of a perfectly safe boat and walk to Him on the water. Impulsive Peter—the disciple who spoke before he thought, the one who acted and then considered the consequences—came when Jesus said, "Come." Without a thought of self-preservation, he jumped out of the boat and started walking on the water.

And then he got to that place. He reached the place like I did on the rock wall . . . that place where he didn't know why he started to do what he was doing in the first place. I'm sure the thought ran through his mind, *Why didn't I just stay in the boat?*

I'm glad Peter didn't stay in the boat. I'm glad he made the radical and unpopular choice to forsake the safety of the boat because the Master was calling. What a great choice. Yes, he sank. Yes, he had to be saved by the Master. But the point is, he was the only one of 12 who was willing to actually get out of the boat and into the storm when the Master called.

How about you? When Jesus calls you to take the risk of sharing your faith, when He calls you to step out of your comfort zone and be Christlike in front of people who aren't, are you willing to step out of the boat? Are you willing to risk a little discomfort in order to answer the call of the Master?

Father in heaven, give me courage to follow Your lead, even when it makes me uncomfortable. Today, I give You my will. Help me to take that leap of faith that You may call me to today. Amen.

THREE AMIGOS

"I am not ashamed of the gospel, because it is the power of God for the salvation of everyone who believes: first for the Jew, then for the Gentile."
Romans 1:16.

Ihave a friend who's been a pastor for years. His name is Dan Serns. Pastor Dan is one of those *live out loud* kind of Christians. If you go to a restaurant with him, he will invite everyone he encounters—hosts, servers, cashiers—to church. He's so bold that it's almost uncomfortable. Sometimes I just want to tell him to be quiet and let me eat. To ask Pastor Dan not to share his faith would be like asking him not to breathe. He's not only "not ashamed of the gospel," but he's downright bold about it.

That's how Shadrach, Meshach, and Abednego lived their lives. They lived out loud. You know the story. The three young men were taken hostage to Babylon from their homeland to serve the king. They were given the king's food to eat and boldly refused it. They were the best of their fellow countrymen—physically, mentally, and spiritually. The reason? Everything they did was for the glory of God.

One day the king got a bright (not) idea. He decided to erect a big statue of himself and have everyone bow down to the idol and worship it. Everybody in the kingdom was gathered on the great plain where the idol was. The command went out: "When the music plays, bow down and worship the image. Anyone who doesn't bow down dies."

It was a pretty simple proposition: do or die. You know the story: the music played, everyone bowed down to the idol . . . except for the three amigos. The king's men saw that the boys were still standing while everyone else was on the ground. They were astonished to see the bold defiance. What were they thinking? Were they dumb or just stubborn? The king decided to give them another chance.

Once again the music started to play. But once again the three friends stood their ground. They didn't even try to disguise their open defiance. The king yelled at them, "Hey, you rotten captives! Don't you know that you're gonna die for this? Just bow down, would you?"

No way, no how. They stood their ground. So the king ordered them to be thrown into a fiery furnace. If they weren't going to obey him, he was going to Kentucky-fry them. "Make the fire hotter," he said.

When the fire was white hot, they were thrown into the furnace.

You know, if the story ended right there, it would still be one of the most remarkable stories in the Bible. The absolute boldness of faith displayed by those young men is astounding. They had no guarantee that God would perform any kind of lifesaving miracle on their behalf. But that didn't factor into their decision to stand up for what they believed. *They were just convicted that it was better to obey God than man, even if their life was on the line.*

I once heard this question: "What if when everyone was bowing down, the three friends decided to bend down and tie their shoes? They wouldn't have been bowing down or anything, they just would have been tying their shoes, right?"

Not these young men. They were not ashamed of the gospel of Christ. They were living out loud. No silent witness. No conveniently untied shoes. Just radical, in-your-face, crazy God followers.

So what about you? When the going gets tough, how do you respond? When your friends are acting outside of the circle of Christ, do you just conveniently go along, or do you stand up for your faith? When you are put in situations that call for you to stand up for your faith, do you have the strength of conviction to stand tall for God, or do you find yourself slinking to the floor to tie your shoes?

All of us have had our times of strength and weakness, but just in case you have found yourself "tying your shoes" more than you need to, here are some suggestions:

1. Start each day by asking God to give you strength in your convictions.

2. Take small steps of boldness. For instance, if you don't already, silently bow your head and thank God for your food, even if you are not with a group of people who do the same.

3. And finally, don't be discouraged if you don't stand up for your faith every time. Just like a physical muscle, your faith gets stronger when you exercise it. The more you live out loud, the bolder you will be in sharing your faith.

God, help me to stand in the face of adversity. Help me to stand up for what I believe in even though it may be uncomfortable or embarrassing. Help me to honor You so that You can look at me and say, "Well done, My good and faithful servant." Amen.

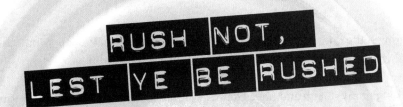

RUSH NOT, LEST YE BE RUSHED

"Be completely humble and gentle; be patient, bearing with one another in love."
Ephesians 4:2.

When our son was born, I had great visions of how he was going to master everything he tried the first time. I was sure he was going to be potty trained at 4 months old, eating solid food at the ripe old age of 3 weeks, and speaking several languages by the time he was 3 years old. My dreams continued. He would also play the piano at age 3, putt like Tiger Woods by 6 years old, and work on the transmission of my truck by the age of 9. I had it all laid out.

Of course, none of these dreams and aspirations came true. In fact, there were times I wondered if my kid was going to pick up on regular everyday kinds of things. But one thing's for sure, I love to celebrate the little triumphs of his life no matter when they happen.

As I write this chapter, I'm sitting in an airplane next to my son and wife, still glowing with pride over his last accomplishment.

For some reason my son developed a healthy respect (intense fear) for water at a very early age. While his peers were swimming and diving under the water, he had to have a floatation device buckled, strapped, and otherwise duct-taped to his body before he'd even lean toward the water. And he had no interest whatsoever in learning how to conquer his fear. If my wife or I would attempt to take him on our back or shoulders into water deeper than four feet, he'd get this frightful panicked look on his face and start screaming (kind of like me when I get my cell phone bill). So, knowing that we were going to be staying on a beach in Penang, Malaysia, this trip, we brought his life jacket with us.

On our way to Penang we had an overnight stop in Singapore, and we stayed in a hotel that had a pool on the roof. My wife and son changed into their bathing suits and headed up to the roof to check the pool out. Without thinking, they left Cole's life jacket in the room. I was napping when they burst through the door 45 minutes later. "Dad, Dad! Guess what? I can swim!" The shear triumph that was beaming from his face was incredible.

"Dad, come on! You've gotta see!"

I put my suit on and traveled up the elevator with him. Without hesitation he ran and jumped in the pool and dog-paddled his way around the water like a newborn seal. What a day!

On this same trip we met Loretta while speaking at the Adventist Hospital in Penang, Malaysia. She's a young nurse with a sweet temperament. Loretta and some of her friends joined us one afternoon by the swimming pool at our hotel. We were all in the pool having a great time when we noticed that Loretta was sticking to the shallow end of the pool. Even my newly swimming son was over in the deeper water with us. I yelled over for Loretta to come join us. She politely declined. She knew how to swim, but at some point in her young life, she had been forced into deep water and had almost drowned. Because of her experience, she was afraid to swim in water that went over her head.

It was amazing what occurred that day. Little by little, on her timetable, we surrounded Loretta with the safety of friends who could swim. Without pressuring her, by the end of the day she was able to swim the length of the deep end of the pool.

There is something to be said about letting people accomplish things on their own timetable. This is especially important in how we look at ourselves in God's kingdom.

Have you ever wondered if you are ever going to be a better person? Have you ever wondered if you are ever going to conquer a bad habit or be a little braver with your faith? And then you look around and see people who seem to have it "all together," and you think, *I'll never get to that level.*

Let me encourage you in two directions:

1. Don't mistake other people's timetable for God's timetable for your life. How long did it take for many of the heroes of the Bible to mature in their faith? It took Samson his whole life. Abraham was 100 years old and still laughing at God's will. Peter had walked around with Jesus for three years, and he still didn't get it. Yet with all of these men God was patient. Remember, it is God's job to help you grow up. It's your job to follow Him as best you can.

2. If God has a lot more work to do on you, then you should be patient with other people, because He's got a lot of work to do on them also. Don't try

to force anyone to be on a spiritual plane that you think they ought to be. That will only produce frustration and fear on their part. It's like the old proverb "Don't try to teach a pig how to sing. It will only frustrate you and annoy a pig." Let God work with others as He has worked with you.

Jesus, help me to learn to wait on You. Please forgive me when I'm impatient with myself and others. Help me to realize that Your plan for my life takes time. Thank You for caring enough about me to take things slowly. Thank You for being patient with me. Amen.

GOAT HEADS

"The evil deeds of a wicked man ensnare him;
the cords of his sin hold him fast."
Proverbs 5:22.

My son just learned how to ride a bicycle. This has been an exhilarating experience for him, but not so much for me. Don't get me wrong—I've enjoyed watching him race up and down the street on his cool-looking bike with his Spiderman helmet. I love watching him grow in confidence as he goes faster and takes more risks. The reason I haven't enjoyed his new bike riding experiences has nothing to do with any of these things. The reason I'm unhappy with his bike riding has to do with goat heads.

Do you know what a goat head is? If you live in a dry area of the world, you might know what a goat head is. No, I'm not talking about the actual head of a goat. I'm talking about the little knobby thorny seed pods that have two little spikes sticking out of them. I'm talking about the most wretched little piece of plant life on Planet Earth. They stick in anything that has the potential to be punctured. They stick to skin (and it hurts!); they stick to the bottom of your shoes; but most of all, they love to stick in bicycle tires. Goat heads pop tires! And guess who has to buy a new inner tube, take the bike apart, and repair the old inner tube? Not the 7-year-old boy—the dad. Grrrrrrr. I hate goat heads.

The way to avoid goat heads in your tires is to stay on the pavement. But my son, learning new and adventurous ways to ride his bike, says, "Dad, I love riding off-road!" which to him means riding on the side of the road through all the weeds and goat heads.

Every time we ride bikes I tell him, "Cole, don't ride off the pavement, or you will get goat heads in your tire and all the air will seep out."

Typically he says, "I know, Dad. Come on, let's just ride!"

So we do. We ride around the neighborhood, and it never fails. He starts off with good intentions. He's gonna stay on the pavement and avoid the goat heads. But sooner or later, time and time again, my son can't resist the feeling of riding "off-road."

By the time I see him head through the thicket on the side of the road it's too late. We usually get home just as his tires are losing their last gasps of air.

The funny thing is that each time this happens my son looks at all the goat heads in his tires and gets upset. "Dad, now I can't ride my bike! I shouldn't have ridden through the goat heads!"

Goat heads are a lot like sin. We know that we get ourselves in all kinds of trouble if we do things that God doesn't want us to do. But sometimes as we ride along in life, we end up seeking a thrill that will always leave us with a feeling as empty as a tire. We get stung with a goat head every time we wander away from God's will. It happens every time. And each time we get mad at ourselves for falling for the same old tricks. I hate goat heads.

Thankfully, we don't have to fall for the same old tricks every time. God sent Jesus and gave us His Word to guide us along the roads of life so that we can avoid the goat heads. And God promises us that when we wander off the road He will forgive us and encourage us to get back on our bike and start pedaling again. We don't have to live life with flat tires if we have Jesus beside us!

Dear Father, keep me from sinning. Lead me away from temptation. Teach me how to avoid situations that lead me to dishonor You. Keep me away from the goat heads in my life. Amen.

PERFECTLY GOOD AIRPLANE

"'Come,' he said. Then Peter got down out of the boat, walked on the water and came toward Jesus."
Matthew 14:29.

There have been times in my life that have necessitated secrecy. I don't keep secrets because I'm a rogue spy for an upstart government agency. I sometimes keep secrets because if my wife finds out what my plans are she won't let me have any fun. Let me give you an example.

When we were first married, Wendy and I had some character-revealing talks. We shared our hopes and fears, our dreams and aspirations. One of my aspirations was to strap a parachute to my back and jump out of an airplane. Wendy wasn't amused. She instructed me, "These are the things that people do when they are single. Married people don't do these kinds of things." I nodded but didn't make any promises.

It was during our third year of marriage that I saw something interesting in our local paper. It was an ad for skydiving for only $65. I clipped the advertisement out and met with my youth group. "Hey, you guys want to go parachuting?" I knew what the answer was going to be. Teenage boys and girls have little to no sense of long-term thinking. They have no sense of their own mortality. Of course they responded with a unanimous "Yes!"

I said, "OK, we can go on just two conditions: (1) you need to get permission from your parents, and (2) you can't tell my wife until after we go."

They all pinky swore that they would keep my dirty little secret. So, on a Sunday that my wife had plans to be out of the house for most of the day, I met with about 30 parents and youth group members and caravanned to the local airport to go jump out of an airplane.

When we got to the airport, I started to wonder what I had gotten myself into. First of all, the only buildings on the property were two trailers on the side of a grass runway. Around one of the trailers there was a rickety wooden deck.

As we pulled up, a man with long hair, dark sunglasses, and more tattoos than an NBA player walked out to greet us. I thought, *What kind of idiot would respond to an ad in the paper advertising skydiving on sale*? Evidently I was that idiot.

With a French Canadian accent our host announced that the first order of business was for each person in our group to sign a waiver. This might not sound like a big deal to you, but as I read what I was signing, I really started to wonder if I was leading my youth group down a path of no return! One of the lines on the waiver said, "If you jump out of our airplane and your parachute doesn't open, we are not liable in any way."

As if that wasn't frightening enough, the next line said, "If you jump out of our airplane and your parachute doesn't open, and you land on any of our stuff, you are liable to pay us for the stuff your dead body breaks." Despite the warnings on the waiver, we all signed on the dotted line and paid the instructor.

As we were being fitted for our jumpsuits, I noticed the men rolling and folding our parachutes into the packs. They all looked like they had been up all night partying after a hard day's work operating rides at the carnival. Not a reassuring sight.

We were finally escorted into another trailer, sat on some wooden benches, and shown a movie. The movie taught us all the things that can go wrong with your parachute after you jump out of an airplane. It also showed us how to operate a parachute if per chance it were to open up correctly.

After about four hours of training, one of the guys said, "OK, I think they are ready!" *We're ready*? A teenager has to log hours behind the wheel and take days of driver's education before they can drive. If you want to serve soda at a fast-food restaurant, you have to study, take a test, and get a physical exam to make sure you don't have a disease. And four hours watching scary movies in an old trailer on the side of a grass runway qualifies me to jump out of an airplane at 3,000 feet? I didn't feel ready.

We were split up into groups of four. I volunteered to go with the last group. (I was just being polite.) The first group boarded the plane and took off. Within a few minutes the plane reached the desired altitude, and one by one each group member jumped out of the airplane and floated like a colorful bubble back down to earth.

Finally it was my group's turn. As we got into the plane, I noticed that I was closest to the door. Everyone who had gone before me was cheering my group as we got into the plane. We took off and climbed to 3,000 feet. The woman sitting in the seat adjacent to me said, "OK, get out of the plane and stand on the peg under the wing! Then jump when I tell you to jump!"

I obeyed. I got out of the airplane, stood on the peg, and held on to the crossbar under the wing. Then I looked down. It was a long way down. I started to think. *What if my parachute doesn't open? What if when I jump, the tail of the airplane hits me in the spleen? What if*... Suddenly my "what ifs" were interrupted by a hard slap on my rump and a voice saying, "Jump!"

I responded, "NO!"

"Jump!"

I had to think. Was I ready to die? Other than keeping this skydiving secret from my wife, I thought so. So I jumped. And I was so afraid, I blacked out.

When a parachute is strapped to you, the straps are wrapped tightly around your chest, over your shoulders, and between your legs. I think this is done so that if you pass out after you jump, the jolt of the parachute opening will wake you up. It did.

I looked up. My parachute was opened! I looked down. The earth was a long way away! And the airplane wasn't coming back! I pulled down on the toggles that held my forward progress and released the chute so that I could sail back to earth.

What a great experience. I don't know that I've ever heard so much quiet and experienced that much fun all at the same time. I landed on the runway to the cheers of those who had gone before me.

After everyone had shed their jumpsuits and all the "First Jump" certificates were signed, we all sat on the deck outside the trailer and shared our glory stories about how we felt jumping out of the plane and how exhilarating it was to sail back down to earth.

That's when I noticed a few of our group sitting on the outside of the circle kind of staring off into the distance. These were the people who had signed the waiver, taken all the training, gone up in the airplane, and hadn't jumped. For some reason they just hadn't been able to do it. And while the rest of the group was sharing their stories, hooting and laughing, they sat and tried to feign joy and enthusiasm for an experience that they had never quite had.

I've met so many people who have done all the right things. They've been to church all their lives. They've been baptized. They've served on committees. Some of them have been preaching and pastoring for a good long time. They've done all these things, but they've never taken that leap of faith, that jump from the safety of their comfort zone, and taken a risk for Christ. A Christian researcher recently polled Christians and has found that upward of 85 percent of professed followers of Christ have never led another person to Jesus.

They've taken all the classes. They've been to all the weekend Bible studies. They've paid their tithe. They've done it all! They've been up in the airplane. But they have never found the courage to jump.

I once had a discussion with a church member about this. We were sitting in a restaurant when I asked him this question: "Why haven't you invited someone to church before? You are a great guy that everyone likes. Why haven't you used that influence to bring some of your friends or business contacts to church?"

He said, "Because it's so uncomfortable. I don't want to mix church with the rest of my life. Besides, you don't just ask someone to church. It's more complicated than that."

"Really," I said. Just then our server came to the table. I asked her, "Hey, do you go to church?"

"No. But I used to when I was a little girl."

"If I invited you to come to church with me and my friend this weekend, would you come?"

"Yeah, sure, I guess. Why not? I could use it."

She met us at the door that very weekend. Did it take courage to ask her? Yep. Was it worth it? Yep.

Why not take a leap of faith? Why not jump? Jesus' last words, the words He left His disciples with before He went back to the Father, were pretty much the same as those of the woman in the airplane. She said, "Jump!" Jesus said, "Go! Make disciples."

It's the same command. It's asking us to get out of our comfort zone and do something that doesn't come natural. It's a risk. But on the other end of the risk is a reward that could have eternal consequences for the people whom we come in contact with.

Oh, and yes, my wife did find out. She forgave me. (But she didn't know that I was going bungee jumping two months later!)

Father in heaven, give me the presence of mind to rely on You in every circumstance, even if it's frightening to me. When I can't see the end from the beginning, help me to know that You are in charge of my life and my calling. Help me to take the leap of faith and not shrink away from the person You've called me to be. Amen.

DISAPPOINTMENT

"I do not understand what I do.
For what I want to do I do not do, but what I hate I do."
Romans 7:15.

A few years ago I was talking about a backpacking trip I was planning to British Columbia, and a friend of mine overheard me. Immediately Ken broke in to my conversation and said, "I wanna go on that trip. That's what I need to do. I need to get away from the phone and all this business and go fishing. Is there fishing?"

I assured him that there was fishing. So plans were set, and four good friends, all pastors (a recipe for a backpacking disaster if there ever was one), set out from Seattle to beautiful British Columbia. Halfway to our destination we stopped in a little town called 100 Mile House so Ken could purchase the fishing gear that would somehow make his trip complete. I don't want to tell you how much he spent on fishing gear that day, but let's just say Ken was late on his rent for the next two months. He was dreaming of pulling five-pound trout out of the lake with every cast.

The backpacking on this trip was a bit rugged. We took two days to hike 13 miles, leading us to Turner Lake, the first of a chain of lakes that we would canoe and portage. Finally we got to our destination, Widgen Lake. Widgen has beautiful sandy beaches hidden under the most jagged-peaked, glacier-littered mountains I've ever seen. The reflection on the still morning waters was breathtaking. In fact, at times the reflection was so pure that some of the pictures we took challenged us as to what was right side up and upside down.

The trip was filled with all kinds of highlights. One day as we sat in our canoes in the middle of a lake we witnessed the amazing sight of two bald eagles fighting in midair, screaming at each other like a couple of angry alley cats. Another fun highlight happened when our friend Alex was bathing in the lake. A deer walked down to the edge of the water where Alex had left his clothes and started biting and nuzzling the shirt and sweat pants like a kitten with a ball of yarn. We got another laugh when at the end of the trip Ken was standing by the fire repeatedly pulling up his pants. (A trip like this really helps shed the pounds.) Finally, out of sheer irritation, he let his pants fall to his ankles. He then stepped out of them and threw them in the fire. "If I can't wear 'em, I'm not hauling 'em back down this mountain."

All of these were great memories, but none of them can top what was the funniest, most tragic memory of them all. The first day up at Widgen Lake we set up camp and cooked supper, anticipating the early-morning rise when we could go fishing. Of course, being excited the night before and getting up early are two totally different emotions. While Ken and I slept in, Jeff and Alex went out early and caught a mess of beautiful cutthroat trout. That morning Ken and I had a rude awakening. Jeff opened our tent and slapped four or five slimy trout on our sleeping bags.

Ken shot up like a bullet. I've never seen a man get dressed so fast. "Alex, come on, I gotta go fishin'!"

Ken gathered his brand-new fishing gear, got in the canoe with Alex, and started paddling to "where the fish were biting."

I wasn't there, so I can only repeat what Alex told Jeff and me later that morning. Ken and Alex paddled to the mouth of a feeder stream, the perfect hideout for large feisty trout. Ken got the new rod and reel in his hand and, like a professional angler, cocked the reel and with one hand snapped the lure back for a perfect cast. As he brought the rod forward, the lure whizzed ahead—as did the rod and reel—right into the lake. That's right, on his first cast, Ken accidentally threw his new rod, reel, and lure into the deep part of Widgen Lake. Alex started to laugh and then, valuing his still-young life, bit his lip and stayed silent.

They paddled to the nearby shore where Ken commandeered a large branch from a pine tree that he used to try to dredge his sunken treasure up. But the lake was too deep.

When they got back to camp, Jeff and I had started breakfast. When we saw them, I said, "Hey, you guys catch anything?"

Ken said, "Shut up."

Behind him Alex motioned that we needed to change the subject and talk about something else. The look on Ken's face that morning can be described in only one word—*disappointment*.

Disappointment is the one human experience we all have in common. We've all experienced it on so many different levels that we've almost come to expect it. And at our core, when we look in the mirror, we have to admit that disappointment is the word that can sum up our human experience as much as any other.

Oh, we have lofty goals, but by the end of the day, we realize that we aren't in the kind of shape we want to be in—physical, mental, social, or spiritual. Truly, we have disappointed ourselves as much as anyone in our life has come to disappoint us.

I'm not the father and husband I want to be. I could stand to lose 15 pounds. This book should have been done last year. I could add more to this list. The point is that I'm disappointed in myself.

One of the teachers in the school of which I'm the principal has a sign in her office that says, "Lord, help me to be the kind of person that my dog thinks I am." The fact of the matter is that none of us will ever be the kind of person that our dogs think we are. No matter whom our dog thinks we are, reality tells us that we all share Paul's experience: "I do not understand what I do. For what I want to do I do not do, but what I hate I do" (Romans 7:15).

When I was a kid, if I expressed disappointment in something, my dad would express this truth: "Get used to it, kid."

Well, the truth is I don't want to get used to it. The problem with disappointment is, well, it's so disappointing.

Disappointment is the reason I am a Christian. Christianity is all about hope. Hope for a brighter future, hope for a better life. Yes, the hope of Christianity is the hope of heaven someday. But I'm more interested in what God can do in my life today, right now. I want to be changed into something better than I am. In fact, if I don't somehow become better than I am, I'm not sure that following Christ is even worth it. Why be a Christian if I'm not going to become more loving, more gracious, more merciful, more self-controlled, and more better (all the English teachers I ever had just rolled over in their graves—more better?). But yes, I want to be more better! I want to experience less disappointment in myself.

I love the words Paul uses to describe the long-term solution to the disappointment he had in himself, "Thanks be to God—through Jesus Christ our Lord! So then, I myself in my mind am a slave to God's law, but in the sinful nature a slave to the law of sin. Therefore, there is now no condemnation for those who are in Christ Jesus, because through Christ Jesus the law of the Spirit of life set me free from the law of sin and death" (Romans 7:25-8:2).

To live in an atmosphere of no condemnation for my shortcomings frees me up to become more of who Christ has called me to be. To become a better father, a better husband, a better principal, and a better person is my deep desire, but it is also God's calling for my life. Walking in the light of His grace, with intention, allows me to become more of this person I want to be.

Do I still get disappointed in myself? Yes. But that's OK. I may cast my fishing gear into the lake every once in a while, but I still stand in the light of God's grace. I still strive to be the person He has called me to be. And I still hang on to the hope that He will mold me into the man that He has called me to be.

Lord, thank You for looking at me, not with disappointment, but with love. Thank You for looking at me as perfect in Your Son. Thank You for seeing me with "no condemnation," but with love and admiration. Amen.

FREEDOM

"But the man who looks intently into the perfect law that gives freedom,
and continues to do this, not forgetting what he has heard, but doing
it—he will be blessed in what he does."
James 1:25.

In one of the most renowned speeches in American history, Patrick Henry shouted the words "Give me liberty or give me death!" I've thought those words. Of course, my motives weren't as noble or my thoughts as pure as Patrick Henry's, but I was almost as sincere.

Because my mother and father both worked, my house became the hangout for a lot of the neighborhood kids after school. Every day after school my friends and I would sit in my living room and watch old *Three Stooges* reruns. Then, after Moe poked Larry in the eye and hit Curly on the head with a frying pan one last time, we'd turn the TV off and figure out what else to do. Most of the time we did productive things, such as play basketball or kickball. Sometimes we'd even have a rousing pinecone fight.

For some reason, on this day, we decided against most of these "productive" activities and decided that we were bored. There is nothing more dangerous than a roomful of unsupervised bored preteens. As we sat and mulled over our options, one of my friends picked up my cat and started highlighting her white fur with an orange highlighter he found next to our phone.

Before long, Adorable (my cat) was a long-haired Persian with bright-orange tips. She didn't seem to care (cats rarely do), so Tim started coloring my dog. When he got done with the dog, he said, "Hey, let's go into the neighborhood and paint all the animals!" So we did. We got all the markers (and some spray paint) that we could find and walked down the street capturing all the unsuspecting dogs and cats. Each one was released after having gone through an extreme makeover.

It wasn't until that evening that I felt the effect of our afternoon artistic foray. There was a knock on our door around suppertime. My dad answered the door. It was Rulph Barren, our neighbor from two doors down. Rulph didn't look very happy. In his hands was his dog, Hussle. Hussle was a terrier mix that used to be black and white. Now Hussle was black and green. In a thick German accent, Rulph let my dad know how unhappy he was with his neon dog. My dad apologized for my behavior (again) and shut the door.

"Did you do this?" he asked. I was going to lie, but our "orange" cat scampered across the room.

"Yes, I did. I didn't think it was that big of a deal, though."

"Well, it is. How many dogs did you do this to?"

"I don't know, maybe 15."

As we were talking, we received several phone calls from neighbors who owned blue-tipped dalmatians, bright-red Jack Russells, and purple mutts. By the time the night was over, I knew I was in trouble.

Finally my dad said, "Son, you are restricted to the house with no visitors for two weeks. You are to have no visitors, no phone calls, no TV, and most of all, no fun!"

I was feeling as though I was being treated unfairly. So I said what I was feeling. "Dad, give me liberty or give me death!"

"Don't tempt me," he said.

My freedom was never so valuable as when I lost it. Freedom is the ultimate desire of every human being. Deep down, each of us cherishes our freedom. And every once in a while, when we catch ourselves in a situation in which our freedom is taken from us, we cherish it all the more.

The book of James calls God's law the law that gives freedom. Talk about an oxymoron! How can something restrictive give me liberty? That's like saying, "This straitjacket will help you be more mobile." The law gives me freedom?

First, let's get away from the word "law" for a moment and substitute it with the words "God's will." For Christians, God's will is expressed profoundly in the Bible, the Word of God. From the Ten Commandments to the life of Christ, we have example after example of what it means to be a God follower. In fact, 100 percent of the *character*-based decisions we have to make in our lives have direct and distinct direction from the Word of God.

So how does God's will give us freedom? In a couple of ways:

1. Jesus said that "I have come that they may have life and have it to the full" (John 10:10). Jesus also said that He wants us to follow God's will and that if we love Him we will keep His commandments (see John 14:15). It stands to reason that if we live by the principles that Jesus has asked us to, our life will be more abundant than it would be otherwise.

2. God knows that when we gamble with our lives by living outside the bounds of His Word, we jeopardize our freedom. I've seen too many cases in which people expressed their "freedom" by engaging in behaviors contrary to God's Word. Whether they experienced tragedies in broken relationships, addiction, or a life of greed, each of them rolled the dice with their lives by seeking "freedom" by choosing behavior contrary to the fence of protection that God's will provides us as expressed in His Word.

3. God's will gives us the freedom to express ourselves and our lives in ways that are free of fear and condemnation. We can truly be ourselves while we stand in the light of His presence. And isn't that what we want, the freedom to be who we were created to be?

Dear Jesus, thank You for giving me freedom from sin, freedom from fear, and freedom to live a life worthy of my calling. Thank You for giving me the Bible as a guideline to keep me free. Amen.

TUNA CASSEROLE

"There is a time for everything, and a season for every activity under heaven."
Ecclesiastes 3:1.

When I was growing up, I loved my mom's cooking. I'm not sure that it was particularly healthy all the time, but it was good. Her lasagna required special tools just to cut the stringy melted cheese as we guided it to our plates. Her potato salad had just the right combination of mayo, mustard, and relish. Her waffles were made from scratch and could put IHOP out of business. But her pièce de résistance, her masterpiece, was her tuna casserole.

Anytime Mom gave me the choice of what we could have for a special dinner, my answer was always the same—tuna casserole. In fact, I was sure that it must have been tuna casserole that was hanging on the tree of knowledge of good and evil. Tuna casserole was the only thing that could ever have temped Adam and Eve to give up the garden.

Once when my sister and my mom left for a mother/daughter weekend, my mom asked, "What would you like me to make you so that you won't starve this weekend?"

Before she could finish her question, I blurted out, "TUNA CASSEROLE!"

I was so excited! Not only did I get the whole house to myself for the weekend, but I was going to get a whole tuna casserole! I didn't have to share the precious manna with anyone!

The next day I didn't eat breakfast. I was preparing my stomach for the onslaught of heavenly food. I turned on the oven to heat up my *chicken of the sea* delicacy. Finally, when the timer went off, I pulled the dish out of the oven and took the foil off. The cheesy tuna aroma made my knees weak. I couldn't wait for the first mouthful of bliss.

I piled my first helping high on the plate and managed to put it down the hatch in record time. I was on a feeding frenzy. I was shoveling it in as fast as I could chew. And when my plate was empty, I filled it again. I was like a hyena over a carcass. My elbows and a fork were flying, and before I knew it, it was gone.

I had eaten the whole tuna casserole in one sitting. And then I heard it. It sounded like the bubble that comes up in the office water jug after somebody pours a drink. Gurgle, gurgle, gurgle. And then I felt the rumble that can be described only as thunder down under.

I started to run for the bathroom. What I had managed to put down so quickly was now intending to come up—more quickly and with quite a bit more force.

When the storm was over, I found myself curled up in the fetal position in front of our toilet, whimpering like a stranded puppy on the side of a busy freeway. I was crying, convulsing, throwing up, and praying for the sweet peace of death all at the same time. All because I took something good to a dangerous extreme.

God wants us to have good things. He wants us to enjoy our life. He also knows that to live a sustained joyous life is to live a balanced life. Whoever came up with the list of seven deadly sins included gluttony as one of them. But eating too much tuna casserole isn't the only way to live a life out of balance.

I know people who spend their whole day texting their friends, talking on the phone, and staying "connected," only to be out of touch with the world around them. I know people who spend too much time at work, making their family life out of balance. I know people who are so wrapped up in making money that they can't meet another person without thinking that they could use them to help attain their goal. I know people who are so into sports that they will sacrifice their church life to stay home and watch a game on television.

In Ecclesiastes it says, "Don't be overrighteous, and be no earthly good. And don't be overwicked; why die before your time? A wise man avoids all extremes."

So what about you? Are you in balance? Here's a test. Ask three close friends or family members to answer this question honestly for you: "Is there any part of my life that's out of balance?"

Take their answers to God and ask Him to give you the balance that you may need to be closer to Him.

Dear Father, make me a more balanced person. Tell me where my life
needs to be more in harmony with Your will. Amen.

YOU NEED YOUR SKIN

*"I praise you because I am fearfully and wonderfully made;
your works are wonderful, I know that full well."*
Psalm 139:14.

Bodies are weird. Well, at least my body is weird. It's a combination of beautiful- and funny-looking parts that, when all assembled, make up a six-feet-six-inch, slightly overweight, slightly uncoordinated man that looks back at me in the mirror every morning.

All my life I've been an above-average athlete, which has given me a false sense of invulnerability in my mid-40s. For some reason I'm not smart enough to realize that the things my mind remembers doing don't necessarily match the things my body is capable of doing now.

In sports my legs and arms refuse to cooperate the way they used to. Recovering from injuries takes twice as long as it did in my 20s. In fact, I'm just now recovering from an injury that I sustained 12 months ago doing a not-so-smart thing in my backyard.

Let me tell you about my experience. After moving into our new house, we discovered two screens that didn't quite fit in the windows they were placed in. One of them was in our master bedroom, and the other was in a bathroom above the back deck. So instead of doing the sensible thing and hiring an agile teenager to do the job, I borrowed an extended ladder from our school and tried to do it myself. After all, what risk could there be in a slightly overweight, slightly uncoordinated man on an extended ladder?

The master bedroom screen was a snap. I set the ladder in my front yard, climbed up, placed a metal spatula under the screen edge, and snapped it into place. No sweat.

The back window was a little trickier. I had to set the ladder on my deck, climb up a steep little mini roof that extends over our porch, fix the window, and then climb back down.

I got up the ladder without a problem. The roof was kind of scary, but I was able to reach the stubborn screen. I was able to get it partway in and figured I needed to go inside the house to finish the job.

As I placed my 230-pound frame on the ladder, it slid quickly out from under me, sending me toward the ground at an alarming rate of speed. I fell about 10 feet, landing back first on my deck railing. From there I fell another eight feet to the ground, landing on my head and left shoulder. And finally, to lend insult to injury, on the way down my foot got caught in the rungs of the ladder. As I toppled to the ground, the ladder followed like a bad habit and landed on top of my already-bruised-and-bleeding body.

Like I said, it's been a year and I'm still healing.

As I write this chapter, I'm sitting in the front seat of an MCI bus filled with junior high students as we leave one of the most unusual exhibits I've ever been witness to. It was called *Bodies: The Exhibit*, and it is a controversial (to some) exhibition of human bodies, pealed, dissected, disassembled, and otherwise displayed to anyone who wants to pay $30 to see it.

What we saw in the exhibit was no less than astounding. The inner workings of the human body are so complex and flawlessly designed that it's a wonder to me that anyone can chalk our existence up to mere chance.

One part of the exhibit had everything from the body removed except for the brain, the nerves, and the nerve endings. What an incredible sight, to see firsthand how our bodies can feel an eyelash drop on the surface of our skin.

The Bible says that we are fearfully and wonderfully made. After seeing this exhibit, I have to say, "Amen!" Each one of us is made with forethought and designed to be uniquely equipped for service in the kingdom of God. We are made to grow and live strong. He even made it so that we could heal, even after we do dumb things like climb ladders and fall on our heads.

Take some time today to appreciate who God created you to be.

Jesus, thank You for creating me in Your image. In Your eyes
I know that I am special, unique, and one of a kind! Amen.

SPANK YOU VERY MUCH

"And will not God bring about justice for his chosen ones,
who cry out to him day and night? Will he keep putting them off?"
Luke 18:7.

Do you remember the last time your parents punished you? I mean really punished you? Did you deserve it? I did. At least the last time I remember getting something more than a slap on the wrist.

I was probably about 11 years old. My dad had been grumpy for about a week. Of course, I didn't help the situation at all. It was summertime, and I made it known that I would rather be out of the house playing with my friends than sticking around doing my chores. So any chance I got I would slip out unannounced and run off.

This happened three or four times. Each time my dad yelled at me and then made me go do whatever I was avoiding—a mild punishment for the fun I was experiencing with my friends.

One night at the dinner table Dad told me that he expected me to meet him in the garage after supper to help him fix the lawn mower. I told him that I would. I was lying. The whole time I was actually planning on running down to Eddie Osborn's house to climb trees. I figured either Dad would forget or I would get another "yelling at" and that would be that.

As I walked up the driveway that night, I saw Dad sitting on the garage floor with lawn mower parts scattered all over the place. He didn't look happy. He stood up and in an uncomfortably controlled voice said, "Go in the house and wait in your room. When I'm done here, I'm going to come in and give you the worst spanking you've ever had."

I tried to argue, but I knew that I was in for it. I was in some serious trouble. I had chosen my path, miscalculated the consequences, and was doomed to pay the penalty.

My face must have been showing my agony, because when I walked into the house, my mom looked at me and asked me what was wrong. I told her and she said, "Well, sport, you've been asking for it all week."

I slunk to my room, shut the door, sat on my bed, and waited . . . and waited . . . and waited. It seemed as if the longer I waited, the more I hurt—and the spanking hadn't even started yet. I contemplated padding my rear end with towels or a pillow. But I knew Dad would make it even worse if he found out.

I didn't know what to do, so I started to pray. I prayed in earnest. I prayed for the second coming of Jesus. I prayed that He would come in the next 10 minutes. I even looked out my window to see if the sky was rolling back like a scroll. It wasn't.

It seemed like hours before I heard the front door open and slam shut. I could hear Dad start down the hallway. I had no strategy. I was in a jam, and I was going to have to pay. My mom thought that what I was about to receive, I deserved. My sister was overjoyed that I was going to get my just reward. And my dad? My dad was just really mad, and he needed to take it out on my backside.

Finally he entered the room . . . with a stick. He didn't even want to mess with the possibility that I had padded my posterior. He had me drop my pants so that the only thing between me and the stick in his hand was a thin layer of white cotton.

That day I received justice. Actually, that justice lasted for a couple of days (at least my backside thought so).

Dad executed justice that day. He gave me what I deserved. I knew that when Dad got fed up, he stopped yelling and started inflicting pain. I never questioned whether I deserved that spanking or not. I knew that what I received was the due penalty for my sin.

God is described all through the Bible as a "just" God. In fact, one day the book of Revelation says that there will be a great multitude of believers standing on the edge of the sea of glass saying, "Great and marvelous are your deeds, Lord God Almighty! Just and true are your ways, King of the ages!" (Revelation 15:3).

Our God is a God of justice. His expectations for us have never wavered. He has set the bar high. Thank God for Jesus! His forgiveness has earned us the right to be saved. Justice was done on the cross. But justice is not what saves us.

Lord, thank You for promising to one day bring justice upon this world. Until then, help me to be fair with my siblings, parents, friends, classmates, and neighbors. Also, help me to receive instruction and judgment as You would have me to—with a calm spirit. Amen.

ROCK CONCERT

"Judgment without mercy will be shown to anyone
who has not been merciful. Mercy triumphs over judgment!"
James 2:13.

One day Jesus was sitting in the Temple teaching. He was telling stories that were illustrating the kingdom of God and telling people about His Father when He heard a terrible ruckus. The people parted in front of Him like the Red Sea as a group of angry Pharisees dragged a half-clad woman to Jesus, dropping her at His feet.

The Pharisees demanded justice. "The law says that this woman should be stoned to death. What do You say, Jesus?"

Jesus wrote some things in the sand with His finger, straightened up, and said, "Let him who is without sin cast the first stone."

One by one the Pharisees stomped away until Jesus was left with the crowd, His disciples, and the woman.

He asked, "Where are your accusers? Is there nobody here to condemn you?" The word here translated as "condemn" is the same word translated other places as "justice." Jesus was saying, "Isn't there anyone here to carry out justice?"

The woman said, "No one, Lord."

Then Jesus said, "Neither will I condemn you: go and stop sinning."

That is mercy. All through the Bible, God is described as a God of mercy. "But you, O Lord, are a compassionate and gracious God, slow to anger, abounding in love and faithfulness" (Psalm 86:15).

Our God is a God of mercy. Mercy means that you escape justice. It means that you don't get what you deserve. Mercy is good, especially when it happens to us!

A few summers ago I was driving through Montana to Michigan from western Canada with my friend Alex. He was driving as we talked and listened to music. Pretty soon we noticed that some pretty red and blue lights were flashing behind us. When we looked down to see how fast Alex was driving, the speedometer said 105.

The police officer asked us where we were going. Alex answered wisely, "We are a couple of pastors heading to seminary."

The officer looked at us, smiled, and said, "That's one of the best lines to get out of a ticket I've ever heard. Hey, keep it down to about 85, will ya, fellas?"

Justice gives us what we deserve. On the flip side, mercy cuts us a break. Our God is a God of mercy. But mercy isn't what saves us, either.

God in heaven, thank You for having mercy on me, a sinner. I know that sometimes I live my life in a way that deserves less of Your blessings, but You continue to love and bless me anyway. Thank You for that. Amen.

MOOSE NOSTRILS

"For it is by grace you have been saved, through faith—
and this not from yourselves, it is the gift of God."
Ephesians 2:8.

In order to share this next story, I need to share with you the mind-set of the people who Jesus was addressing with this parable.

Pharisees were the religious elite of Jesus' time. They dressed differently than the world, they ate differently than the world, and they thought of themselves as separate from the world. In fact, ancient Jewish texts tell us that the Pharisees had a nickname for themselves. They called themselves "the righteous," a term used to separate themselves from the world. Kind of how some people like to call themselves "the remnant."

These people were so afraid of being unrighteous that they created a whole set of laws around the laws of God that they obeyed, just so they wouldn't even accidentally break a law of God. They were horrified by sin. And they wouldn't be caught dead associating with anyone harboring a known sin. And let me tell you, they knew what sin was.

It was these people, among others, whom Jesus told this parable to. He said, "Once upon a time there was a man who had two sons. One day the younger of the two sons approached his dad and said, 'Dad, I want my inheritance, and I want out of this family.'"

Immediately the Pharisees got moose nostrils (a condition that happens to religious people when they get offended. Their nostrils flare and their eyebrows rise, making them look like a moose.)

They knew what was happening. Inheritances were to be received after a father died, not before. To ask your father for an inheritance while he was alive was tantamount to treating your father as a dead man. This son was asking to die to his family. The appropriate response would have been for the father to tear his clothing and turn his back on this ungrateful son, thus declaring him to be no longer a family member.

But Jesus' story didn't go on the way it was supposed to. He said, "The man gave his son the money, and the son went off to live in a far country."

Again Jesus' listeners got moose nostrils, and they started to grumble. A faraway country? This boy was consorting with Gentiles? Surely the father would disown this boy of his. People who consorted with Gentiles were considered the worst kind of sinners—sinners who could not repent or come back to God. Jesus even described this boy as living an "unsaved life." This kid was in open rebellion. Later he was described as spending his money on filthy things. In fact, the Greek word for what this boy was doing was "pornea," the root of which gives us words in today's vernacular that describe ugly things.

By now the Pharisees were getting sick to their stomachs. What a wretched boy. But the story got worse.

One day, when a famine came and the boy ran out of money, he was forced to go and ask to work for a Gentile. He got a job tending pigs. He even shared their food.

By now the Pharisees had all developed nervous twitches. Not only does the Old Testament forbid the eating of swine's flesh—it curses those who touch it. As Jesus painted the story, the Pharisees realized that there had never been a more sorry case of sin and rebellion than the boy in this story. According to their laws, according to everything they knew about the Bible, this kid was lost beyond all repair.

Then Jesus got a little grin on His face as He continued the story. One day the boy came to his senses and reasoned with himself, "The servants in my dad's house have it better than I do. Even though I'm not worthy of being a son in his household, even though I am dead to my father and he is dead to me, maybe he will have mercy, and hire me as a hired hand."

The Pharisees were on their toes. What would the father do? Would he do justice? Would he show mercy and hire the boy? Or would he do the right thing and not even acknowledge his presence? What would he do?

Jesus continued the story. "While the boy was yet a long way off, the father saw him and ran to him." The Pharisees couldn't believe their ears. It was considered very undignified for a man to run, especially a rich man like the father in this parable.

"The Father ran and threw his arms around the boy." Again the Pharisees gasped. To touch someone who was unclean—what was this father thinking? Who knew what was still on this kid's clothing from the pigpen? What kind of father was this, anyway?

"And then he kissed him." When you read this text in English, it just doesn't do this verse justice. The Greek suggests, "He kissed him and continued to kiss him over and over."

"The father placed a royal robe on his son. Then he reinstated him as a family member by placing the family seal, a ring, on his finger. And finally, despite the kid's request to be hired as a servant, the father, knowing that only servents went barefoot, placed sandals on his son's feet."

Again, the sense that you get from the Greek is that right after that a spontaneous party broke out. It's almost like the party was unavoidable. It just broke out. The barbeque was lit, the fatted calf was killed, and people started to dance with joy.

And the father said, "My son was once dead, but now is alive. He was lost, but now is found."

At the end of the story Pharisees were fainting left and right, because this was *not* how the Father should be represented in a parable.

But what Jesus' listeners failed to see was grace. Justice would have demanded punishment. At least a good scolding. Mercy simply would have dismissed the consequences and taken the kid back as a hired hand. Mercy would have cut the kid some slack. But grace . . . grace throws a party. Grace reinstates. Grace kisses and continues to kiss. Grace clothes in a royal robe.

The Bible tells us this:

"For it is by grace you have been saved, through faith—and this not from yourselves, it is the gift of God—not by works, so that no one can boast. For we are God's workmanship, created in Christ Jesus to do good works, which God prepared in advance for us to do" (Ephesians 2:8-10).

Grace demands a response.

You may be in the process of coming back from a far country. Today, won't you respond to His grace? The Father is running toward you with open arms. He's got a white robe for you to wear; He's got some shoes for your feet (you don't have to be a servent to sin anymore); and He's got the family seal for you, the Holy Spirit. Grace is yours for the taking. Justice was done at the cross. Mercy won't cut it this time. You need grace. I need grace.

Jesus, thank You for grace. Thank You for Your sacrifice.
Thank You for looking at me as though I have never sinned. Thank You
for taking my filthy rags in exchange for a crown. It doesn't seem fair, but
I'll take Your gift with humility and thankfulness. Amen.

BODY SPOTS

"But I say unto you, Love your enemies, bless them that curse you, do good to them that hate you, and pray for them which despitefully use you, and persecute you."
Matthew 5:44, KJV.

It's no secret that my sister and I didn't get along very well when we were kids. We love each other now, but as children we fought like Israelis and Palestinians. And worse than that, we would actually get joyful when something bad or unfortunate happened to the other one.

If I got a spanking, my sister would walk by the door and give me that little facetious look of "Oh, I'm *so* sorry for you." This little rivalry was ever-present.

To compound my misery, sometimes my mom would make me bring my sister with me when I went to do things with my friends in the neighborhood. So I would take every opportunity to get out of having to do that. Consequently, I loved it when she would get sick, because it gave me a chance to play with my friends and not have my "shadow" right there with me.

That's why I couldn't believe the stroke of luck when I noticed something on my sister that I had never seen before. Little red bumps began to form on her legs, arms, and back. She even got several on her face. And they began to itch. My sister had chicken pox.

You can't imagine the joy I felt. And she didn't only have chicken pox; she got mumps at the same time. Not only was my sister going to be out of commission for a couple weeks—I could get a lot of mileage out of making fun of her for looking like a polka-dot hamster storing nuts for the winter. But best of all, I was going to be free of my little shadow to play with my friends as I pleased. Not waiting for her to catch up, no worries about a tattletale, no sharing of friends. Life was good. My joy was complete.

It was a day later that I noticed a little red bump on my chest. Could it be a pimple? Please, God, let it be a pimple. And then I saw another. It began to itch. And then another. By the end of the day they looked like a cluster of itchy inflamed constellations. Life was not good. And then my jaw started to feel a little sore. I looked in the mirror. I had the mumps, too.

Instead of being enemies, my sister and I ended up at home with a babysitter each day, gently rubbing a special lotion on our chicken pox so they wouldn't itch so badly.

The feeling of terror and regret I felt when I looked down and saw that little red bump on my chest was nothing like the feeling of terror and doom that Naaman must have felt the day he looked down and saw what he knew to be the most dreaded disease of his time—leprosy.

The story is found in 2 Kings 5. It starts like this: "Now Naaman was commander of the army of the king of Aram" (verse 1).

In order for this story to have its proper impact, you need to know something about Naaman's hometown. Naaman, as the text says, was from a place called Aram. Aram wasn't just an ordinary town. Israel's history with Aram was as difficult and checkered as it was with any town in the Bible. Isaac's wife, Rebekah, was from Aram. It was to Aram that Jacob fled when he deceived Esau for his birthright. Aram is where Uncle Laban was deceived by Jacob as he sneaked off with Laban's daughters. It was from Aram that the prophet Balaam was sent to curse Israel when they were wandering in the wilderness. In the book of Judges you will find it was the town of Aram that was frequently raiding Israel and causing all kinds of havoc for them. Israel even took some of the foreign gods of Aram and began to worship them. When Solomon was king, one of his chief adversaries, one of the constant thorns in his flesh, was the king of Aram. King Ahab, in fear of the king of Aram, gave the king of Aram all of the gold from the sanctuary of God.

So you can see that up until now, Aram was no vacation destination for Israel. Not only did the people of Israel not like anyone or anything from Aram, but they despised Aram. If they had a nuclear bomb and could set it in the middle of any town and blow it up, they would have chosen Aram. OK, now that we know about the town of Aram, let's continue our story.

"He [Naaman] was a great man in the sight of his master and highly regarded, because through him the Lord had given victory to Aram. He was a valiant soldier, but he had leprosy. Now bands from Aram had gone out and had taken captive a young girl from Israel, and she served Naaman's wife. She said to her mistress, 'If only my master would see the prophet who is in Samaria! He would cure him of his leprosy.'

"Naaman went to his master and told him what the girl from Israel had said. 'By all means, go,' the king of Aram replied. 'I will send a letter to the king of Israel.'

"So Naaman left, taking with him ten talents of silver, six thousand shekels of gold and ten sets of clothing. The letter that he took to the king of Israel read: 'With this letter I am sending my servant Naaman to you so that you may cure him of his leprosy.'

"As soon as the king of Israel read the letter, he tore his robes and said, 'Am I God? Can I kill and bring back to life? Why does this fellow send someone to me to be cured of his leprosy? See how he is trying to pick a quarrel with me!'

"When Elisha the man of God heard that the king of Israel had torn his robes, he sent him this message: 'Why have you torn your robes? Have the man come to me and he will know that there is a prophet in Israel.'

"So Naaman went with his horses and chariots and stopped at the door of Elisha's house. Elisha sent a messenger to say to him, 'Go, wash yourself seven times in the Jordan, and your flesh will be restored and you will be cleansed.'

"But Naaman went away angry and said, 'I thought that he would surely come out to me and stand and call on the name of the Lord his God, wave his hand over the spot and cure me of my leprosy. Are not Abana and Pharpar, the rivers of Damascus, better than any of the waters of Israel? Couldn't I wash in them and be cleansed?' So he turned and went off in a rage.

"Naaman's servants went to him and said, 'My father, if the prophet had told you to do some great thing, would you not have done it? How much more, then, when he tells you, "Wash and be cleansed"!' So he went down and dipped himself in the Jordan seven times, as the man of God had told him, and his flesh was restored and became clean like that of a young boy.

"Then Naaman and all his attendants went back to the man of God. He stood before him and said, 'Now I know that there is no God in all the world except in Israel. Please accept now a gift from your servant.'

"The prophet answered, 'As surely as the Lord lives, whom I serve, I will not accept a thing.'

"And even though Naaman urged him, he refused. 'If you will not,' said Naaman, 'please let me, your servant, be given as much earth as a pair of mules can carry, for your servant will never again make burnt offerings and sacrifices to any other god but the Lord. But may the Lord forgive your servant for this one thing: When my master enters the temple of Rimmon to bow down and he is leaning on my arm and I bow there also—when I bow down in the temple of Rimmon, may the Lord forgive your servant for this.'

"'Go in peace,' Elisha said" (2 Kings 5:2-19).

Can you believe what you just read? Do you see the importance of the story? I don't know that there are many stories in the Bible that illustrate the grace of God so well as the story of a little slave girl, Elisha, and Naaman.

How do you treat your enemies? How do you treat the people that turn your stomach? Do you avoid them? Do you talk poorly about them behind their backs? Or do you pray for them and bless them?

I want you to notice how a little slave girl, a prophet of God, and God Himself treated their archenemy, Naaman, when he needed a little help.

The little slave girl . . . she could have assumed that the Lord was paying her owner back for raiding her town and stealing her by inflicting Naaman with leprosy. Instead, she recognized that God had been gracious to her in her life, so she became a dispenser of grace.

The prophet . . . he could have realized that these were Old Testament times—an eye for an eye and a tooth for a tooth. Naaman had raided and created havoc in the name of the king of Aram for years. This guy was public enemy number one! And besides that, he worshipped foreign gods. He bowed down to idols!

Notice that Elisha didn't even accept a gift from Naaman. Elisha realized that you can't do anything to earn grace. Grace is dispensed as a gift, not as something you can buy or earn.

But shouldn't Elisha have at least straightened Naaman's theology out a little? I mean, come on, thinking that somehow God was in the dirt from Israel? Give me a break. He could have at least had a Bible study with Naaman before he left.

And then when Naaman asked Elisha to bless him and forgive him even though he would still have to go into the pagan temples and worship with his king, Elisha just says, "Dude, don't worry about it—go in peace."

Is that how you treat the man who represents the place you hate the most? Yes. Yes, it is. This is the most important lesson in Scripture, and it is the one we are the slowest to learn.

Jesus opened His mouth on the side of a mountain and said, "Love your enemies and pray for those who persecute you, because you will be forgiven as you forgive and you will be judged as you have judged."

God's people are not called to be judges, nor are they called to be harsh executors of judgment. God's people are to be dispensers of grace.

*Dear Jesus, help me to treat my enemies like You treat Your enemies—
with love and respect. This is not an easy prayer for me to pray, Lord,
but help me to do what You've asked me to do and be who
You've asked me to be, in spite of my feelings. Amen.*

BOLD LITTLE GUY

When I was in high school, I was a big lug who occasionally enjoyed picking on people smaller than I (which was just about everyone). Most of the kids whose lives I made miserable avoided me. If they saw me coming toward them, they'd walk the other way.

This was true of all of them except for one—John Matthison refused to be intimidated by me. Whatever I dished out, John would always come back with a defiant look or comment that kept me a little uneasy. I was a lot bigger than he was, but he wasn't intimidated in the least.

One day I was walking to class and saw John coming toward me. As we approached each other, I made sure that there was no option for him but to walk off the sidewalk into the wet grass.

In the blink of an eye, John dropped his books, lowered his shoulder, and dropped me in the muddy grass, staining my pants.

He got up, looked at me, and said, "You may be bigger than I am, but I'm not afraid of you." Then he walked off. That day John earned my respect, and I stopped picking on him.

That was Elisha. The stuff he was up against often looked big. But he wasn't about to run and hide. He had the attitude toward life that said, "Bring it on!" The story below is from 2 Kings 6:8-23.

"Now the king of Aram was at war with Israel. After conferring with his officers, he said, 'I will set up my camp in such and such a place.' The man of God sent word to the king of Israel: 'Beware of passing that place, because the Arameans are going down there.'

"So the king of Israel checked on the place indicated by the man of God. Time and again Elisha warned the king, so that he was on his guard in such places. This enraged the king of Aram. He summoned his officers and demanded of them, 'Will you not tell me which of us is on the side of the king of Israel?'

"'None of us, my lord the king,' said one of his officers, 'but Elisha, the prophet who is in Israel, tells the king of Israel the very words you speak in your bedroom.'

"'Go, find out where he is,' the king ordered, 'so I can send men and capture him.' The report came back: 'He is in Dothan.' Then he sent horses and chariots and a strong force there. They went by night and surrounded the city. When the servant of the man of God got up and went out early the next morning, an army with horses and chariots had surrounded the city.

"'Oh, my lord, what shall we do?' the servant asked.

"'Don't be afraid,' the prophet answered. 'Those who are with us are more than those who are with them.' And Elisha prayed, 'O Lord, open his eyes so he may see.' Then the Lord opened the servant's eyes, and he looked and saw the hills full of horses and chariots of fire all around Elisha. As the enemy came down toward him, Elisha prayed to the Lord, 'Strike these people with blindness.' So he struck them with blindness, as Elisha had asked. Elisha told them, 'This is not the road and this is not the city. Follow me, and I will lead you to the man you are looking for.' And he led them to Samaria. After they entered the city, Elisha said, 'Lord, open the eyes of these men so they can see.' Then the Lord opened their eyes and they looked, and there they were, inside Samaria.

"When the king of Israel saw them, he asked Elisha, 'Shall I kill them, my father? Shall I kill them?'

"'Do not kill them,' he answered. 'Would you kill men you have captured with your own sword or bow? Set food and water before them so that they may eat and drink and then go back to their master.' So he prepared a great feast for them, and after they had finished eating and drinking, he sent them away, and they returned to their master. So the bands from Aram stopped raiding Israel's territory."

That's quite a story, isn't it? I admire Elisha. I think his life stands as a challenge to us every time we are tempted to throw in the towel, every time we want to give up, every time we want to run from our problems, we need to be reminded of people like Elisha. People who stand in the face of intimidation and say, "Bring it on."

Elisha didn't exact revenge; he killed them with kindness. Proverbs 25:21, 22 says, "If your enemy is hungry, give him food to eat; if he is thirsty, give him water to drink. In doing this, you will heap burning coals on his head, and the Lord will reward you."

Elisha knew that making friends was more valuable than beating an enemy. And I've found that in life every attempt that we can make to live at peace with the people who are out for us is worth it.

I've had several occasions in my life that I had the upper hand on an adversary. Sometimes I struck them hard with words and actions, and sometimes I treated them with compassion and kindness. I've found it's better to make a friend than crush an enemy. I would encourage us to follow Elisha's example. Be bold, and in the process, try to make a new friend.

Dear Father, open my eyes so that I can see how You are with me in the hard times. Give me a glimpse of how Your heavenly host surrounds me to protect me and save me in times of trouble. Amen.

SATAN'S EYEBALL

"He got up, rebuked the wind and said to the waves, 'Quiet! Be still!'
Then the wind died down and it was completely calm."
Mark 4:39.

The church that I interned at had a great ministry. At least those of us who started it thought of it as a ministry. A few folks in church just thought it was an excuse for a bunch of guys in the same church to have fun together.

Through a new member of the church we decided to start a ministry that took groups out for a weekend of worship, praise, great teaching, and white-water rafting down the Wenatchee River! That's right, we'd provide the speaker, the music and the food, a calm nature float, and then a Sunday of wild white-water rafting complete with wet suits, life jackets, and all the necessary equipment that would make a white-water adventure all that it was supposed to be.

We had been down the Wenatchee River lots of times, and I knew well the dangers of each set of rapids. The rapids all had interesting names. There is Drunkard's Drop, Cashmere Schmear, Granny Rapids, The Suffocater, Rodeo Hole, and the first big rapid after the put-in, Satan's Eyeball.

On this day I was to be training a couple of new guides from our church. My instructions were to let the new guys guide and not say anything unless there was an emergency. (Anyone who knows me knows that not saying anything is a challenge that I don't easily live up to.) But I agreed to sit in the boat and keep my mouth shut.

That morning our head guide had a safety talk with all the rafters. He reminded all the guides that our first set of rapids were just around the bend from the put-in, and then we had prayer, asking God for safety from the dangers of the river (and from the new guides).

We put in with a raft full of excited people (including my sister and a friend who were more nervous than excited) and Roy, a guy who worked in the treasury office that signed my paychecks (which made me very nervous).

As we rounded the first bend toward the first series of white-water rapids, we could see the boiling, frothing water just waiting for an eight-man raft to roller coaster its way through them. As we got closer, I noticed that our guides weren't barking out any commands. In fact, we were drifting sideways, with no momentum, toward one of the most notorious rapids in the river, Satan's Eyeball.

I looked back at our trainees to see if I could figure out what their strategy was. All I saw was a couple of people who looked like deer in headlights. But I wasn't supposed to say anything, so I didn't. Satan's Eyeball got closer. I didn't say anything. I looked at my sister, who was looking at Satan's Eyeball. She couldn't say anything. She was terrified by the sight and sound of her pending doom. I still didn't say anything.

Finally I couldn't stand it. We were drifting sideways toward one of the most dangerous holes in the river and nobody was saying anything. There was no warning, no clear command to guide us. We were drifting into the teeth of Satan's Eyeball. Finally, I screamed, "Guys! What are we going to do here!"

My query came too late, and we slid sideways over what can only be described as thunderous, violent confusion. The hydraulic caused by the giant hole sucked half the raft under water and took three of our rafters out in the blink of an eye. Then every guide's nightmare happened. The raft started crawling back up the rapid. Satan's Eyeball was trying to turn the raft over and lose the rest of us into the cold waters of the Wenatchee River.

I was done not saying anything. I screamed, "High side! High side!" The remnant of the sinking ship climbed up the raft to place our weight on the side of the raft that was crawling up the rapid. As we did, the rapid released us.

As soon as we were out of danger, we started looking for the people who had been sucked out of the raft. The powerful backflow had sucked my sister and her friend under the raft. They had managed to find their way out to the sides, bobbing up in the water with eyes wide and mouths gasping for air. We grabbed them and yanked them into the boat. But where was my treasurer? Would I ever get a paycheck again?

Roy, the treasurer, was floating 100 yards downriver toward a dam. I took over the guide position, and we booked it down the river and saved Roy just before the portage. I'm not sure, but I think I had a slight cut in pay after our adventure was over.

Drifting down the river in a boat without a clear command was almost our undoing that day. Equally as dangerous are professed God followers who drift down the river of life without any clear direction. I can't tell you how many Christians I've met that spend no time in the Bible and no time in reflection and meditation. They are drifting down the river of life headed for who knows what, not hearing the clear call of God in their lives to warn them of danger or (even worse, in my opinion) missing out on an adventure that God is just waiting to lead them through.

Why not take some special time each morning to connect with *your* God? Why not spend a little time after prayer to meditate and listen for His voice in *your* life? Why not have the best Guide ever in *your* life raft? After all, even the wind and the waves obey His voice.

Jesus, be my guide. Help me to be so tuned to Your voice that I can pick it out of the loudness of this world. Lead me. Guide me. And please protect me from the rapids of this violent world. Amen.

SHAMU DREAM

"And afterward, I will pour out my Spirit on all people. Your sons and daughters will prophesy, your old men will dream dreams, your young men will see visions."
Joel 2:28.

For most of my life I was generally a pretty happy guy. I didn't usually have big ups and downs or emotional swings. I was just kind of in the middle all the time. It wasn't as exciting as what some people got to live, but I was pretty sure I wouldn't die of a heart attack in my 40s. I just didn't get that worried about stuff.

And then I became a principal.

My fourth year as a principal should have been my happiest year. Our school was in better shape financially, spiritually, and academically than I think it had ever been. I had a group of teachers who were professional, fun, and creative. Most of my parents were on board with the program . . . and then the wheels started to fall off my life. Let me explain.

At the end of my third year the junior high school had to move to make room for the growing elementary section of the school. That move pushed the junior high school across the parking lot into the basement of another building. That didn't make the teachers, students, or parents very happy. To make things worse, this was the year that my junior high students decided to act like junior high students.

As the behavior of the students and the frustration of my teachers started to escalate, some things started happening in my personal life that were probably the result of grief from the death of a young woman who had lived with us, parental oversights, and bad timing. Added to that, a good friend and faculty member whom I had really stuck my neck out for made some poor life choices, which resulted in his resignation and replacement. So, to sum the situation up, at a time when I should have been feeling like the king of my little school administrator world, I was feeling so low that I thought I needed to quit and start a new occupation somewhere far, far from my problems (like that ever works).

To complicate matters even more, when things seemed the most desperate and dark, two things happened that almost always happen to people in ministry at the wrong time. I received several phone calls of people interested in me as either principal or pastor in their town (far away from where I was currently experiencing my personal pain), and some people in my church community starting spreading horrible rumors about my personal situation.

This is where God steps into the story. (Just to be clear, He was always in the story—I just didn't notice it until He stepped up and gave me the hug that I needed Him to give me.)

It was spring break, and I was driving a group of students and sponsors to an orphanage in Mexico on a mission trip. As I crossed the U.S./Mexico border, I turned off my phone.

That very morning Jonny Hisey, my Spanish teacher's husband, woke up visibly disturbed.

"Honey, what's the matter?" Annie asked.

"I just had the weirdest dream," Jonny replied.

"That's really strange—you never dream, much less remember your dreams. What was your dream about?"

"Nothing, really. This guy I've never seen walked up to me and said, 'You need to pray for and encourage Mark Witas.' Then he left. That was it—that was the dream."

"Well?"

"Well what?"

"Are you gonna call him?"

"I hardly know him. No, it was just a silly dream. Why would I call him?"

By now Annie was dialing my cell number and handing the phone to her husband, "Because when God tells you to do something, you do it."

Jonny put the phone to his ear and heard my message. It was obvious to him that my phone was off, but he decided to leave a message of encourage-ment anyway. Then he hung up and forgot about it.

Ten days later I was sitting on a bench at Sea World in San Diego. The students and sponsors were all watching big fish jump through flaming hoops or getting really wet on rides, and my son was in a shop across from where I was sitting looking for more unnecessary stuff to cram into his bedroom. I decided to do what I was trying to avoid, knowing that I was going to have a zillion messages on my phone, most of them things I just didn't want to deal with. I typed in my code. "You have . . . 37 messages; first message . . ."

I saved and deleted messages for a few seconds. About seven messages in, I started to cry. I was listening to Jonny's message of encouragement. It was the most heartfelt, beautiful message I think I've ever heard.

My son came out of the shop and looked at me. "Dad, are you OK? Did you get stung by a bee?"

"No, buddy, I just listened to a really nice message, and it was what I really needed to hear."

"Let's go on the really big ride, Dad. OK?"

"OK, bud, let's go."

We stood up and walked about 20 feet. As I looked up, I couldn't believe my eyes. There, standing right in front of me, were Jonny and Annie Hisey. He saw me and said, "What in the world are you doing here?"

"We stopped on the way back from our mission trip. What are you doing here?"

"We were visiting Annie's parents in Palm Springs, and we decided last night to come to Sea World."

"Jonny, I just listened to the message you left for me on my phone, and it really touched me. Thank you."

"Wow! God told me in a dream to leave that message!"

"What? Really? What are you talking about?" Then Jonny told me the rest of the story.

Sometimes God gives us a hug just when we need it the most.

Spirit, thank You for hugging me when I need it the most. Your presence in my life is comforting and healing. Please use me to "hug" other people, because we are all struggling here on this earth. Use me to touch someone else's life as You continue to touch mine. Amen.

RIDE THAT BANANA

As you've probably guessed by now, I have no business putting anything on my feet but shoes. I have experienced nothing but disaster with ice skates, skis, sailboards, stilts, unicycles, etc.

My history of damaging myself (body and psyche) started at a young age.

When I was 10 years old, the boys in my neighborhood started to get excited about skateboarding. It looked fun. I hadn't yet learned that God didn't create my feet for things other than shoes, so I wanted one.

I asked my dad, "Can I have a skateboard?"

"No, you'll break your head."

"Please?" I begged.

Dad gave in pretty quickly. "OK, we'll get one this weekend."

The weekend rolled around, and my dad kept his promise. We got into the car and headed for town. But he drove by the really super-cool skateboard shop and pulled into the Kmart parking lot. "What are we doing here?" I asked.

"Getting you a skateboard."

"But they don't have good skateboards here."

"I know."

"But I want a good skateboard."

"I'm not spending hundreds of dollars to buy you something that you are going to use for one week and then lose."

"But . . ." We walked through the store until we found the bikes and skateboards. There weren't many to choose from, but we finally decided on a bright-yellow plastic skateboard that looked the best out of the horrible selection on display. It was $19.99. I think we paid about $19 too much.

When we got home, my dad sat me down and warned me, "You can skateboard anywhere you want, but whatever you do, don't skateboard down Sprague Hill. It's too steep, and you'll break your head open. Promise me that you won't skateboard down Sprague Hill."

"I promise."

I ran to Dennis and Tim's house to show them my new board. John and Kenny were there too. When I walked in, they all fell on the ground, held their guts, and belly-laughed, pointing at my new skateboard. Finally Tim choked out, "It's, it's a BANANA! Ha, ha, ha." (Which is what they called my skateboard from that day on: *the Banana.*)

My friends started to teach me how to ride my skateboard. (Remember, these were the days before helmets and protective gear.) I got a little nicked up here and there, but it wasn't anything severe. As I learned, I gained confidence in my abilities. And then I reached the point at which I thought I could ride the Banana anywhere my friends could with their really super-cool expensive skateboards.

One Sunday the guys came over to the house with their skateboards and knocked on my door. When I came out onto my front porch, they looked over their shoulder at my dad working on our car in the driveway and whispered, "Come on, grab the Banana—we're going to do Sprague Hill!"

Promise me you won't ride down Sprague Hill. My dad's words rang in my ears. I knew that if he found out I had gone down Sprague Hill on the Banana, he'd take my skateboard away, and possibly my life. Dad wasn't a big fan of open defiance.

I power-whispered back, "Are you guys crazy? It's too steep. And you guys have really super-cool expensive skateboards. I've got a $19 banana! We'll kill ourselves going down that hill."

They started jerking their heads around and flapping their arms and making chicken noises. They were acting like a bunch of 10-year-olds. Oh yeah, they were 10-year-olds.

"Knock it off, you guys! Fine, I'll go, but I'm only going to watch." (Like I've ever once in my life only watched.)

When we got to the top of Sprague Hill and looked down, it seemed to me that since I had last been there civil engineers had come and somehow made it steeper. It was frightening enough to ride a bike down that hill, but a skateboard? Even my stupid friends weren't that stupid.

Dennis and John hopped on their skateboards. "We'll go down first. If it's safe, then we'll wave you down."

"If it's not, I'll call the ambulance." I grinned.

They started rolling down the hill on their really super-cool expensive skateboards. They looked like angels floating down the hill. There wasn't a wobble or a jiggle. The wind blew through their hair as they sailed down the hill with the greatest of ease.

When they reached the bottom, they jumped off their boards, grinned, and yelled, "Come on, you guys—it was easy!" They waved their arms and beckoned us down the hill.

Tim looked at me and said, "Well, what do you think? Can the Banana take the hill?"

"I don't know. It's pretty steep. And I told my dad I wouldn't take the Banana down Sprague Hill."

"Oh, come on—he'll never know!" As always, these were our famous last words.

"OK, but if anyone tells my dad, I'm toast."

When we started down the first part of the hill, it wasn't too bad. The Banana held steady as it picked up speed.

And then it happened. It started out as a little wiggle. Then it turned into a noticeable wobble. By the time I realized that things were rapidly getting out of my control, the Banana was careening down the hill at a breakneck speed and experiencing some sort of a severe skateboard malfunction. I was faced with two choices: I could fall on the pavement or the grass. The grass looked so much softer.

I decided to try to angle the board toward the grass so that I could jump off the now violently trembling Banana and minimize the physical trauma that I was sure to sustain.

As I did, the wheels of the Banana made contact with some loose pebbles on the road. The Banana sprung toward the grass . . . without me. I hit the pavement and started to tumble like a bad car accident.

I don't know how far I tumbled and skidded down that hill, but when I woke up, my friends all looked like *they* were going to cry. Everything hurt. I was wearing only shorts and a T-shirt, so I looked like I had been through a blender. Blood was pouring down my legs, arms, and shoulders. I had also cut my head open, and blood was pouring into my eyes and down my chin. I was a mess.

My friends picked me up and ever so gently helped me back up Sprague Hill, through a little area of woods and into my neighborhood. When we got to the bottom of my driveway, they saw my dad working on the car, gulped, and scattered.

When Dad looked up, it looked like he saw a ghost. He ran over to me and said, "What happened? Are you OK?" (He knew I wasn't OK! I looked like I'd been attacked by piranhas. That's just what you say when you see somebody that looks like walking raw hamburger.)

I started to cry. "Dad, I went down Sprague Hill. I'm so sorry; I'm so, so sorry!"

He took me in the house and drew a bath. He gently removed what was left of my T-shirt and the rest of my clothes and got me in the bathtub. He took tweezers and pulled out all of the pebbles embedded in my skin. He cleaned my wounds, dried me off, and gently put his special bathrobe around me.

I said, "Dad, what's my punishment for disobeying you? What's going to happen to me for going down Sprague Hill?"

"It already happened," he said. "Mark, I didn't tell you not to go down Sprague Hill because I don't like you; I told you not to do it because I love you and want to protect you from yourself. Sometimes you can't see what I can see as your dad. I wasn't trying to be mean; I was just trying to be a good dad."

Adam and Eve ate the fruit. The punishment was a natural consequence for their sin. I rode the Banana down Sprague Hill. I think I still have rocks embedded in places that are yet to be discovered.

The Bible is our life manual. It tells us how to live. Some people think it's too restrictive and has somehow become outdated for the twenty-first century. They don't realize that God isn't trying to be mean or steal their fun. He's just trying to protect His kids.

Jesus, thank You for my parents. They aren't perfect, but they have given me a glimpse of who You are. Help me to obey my parents and listen to their advice. Thank You for Your protection and guidance. Amen.

SACRIFICE

"Greater love has no one than this, that he lay down his life for his friends."
John 15:13.

When Wendy, Cole, and I moved to Wenatchee, we didn't know what God had in store for us, but we knew that we were open to whomever He placed in our lives. It turns out, He had quite a plan.

My first encounter with Meghan was in the gymnasium at Cascade Christian Academy. I had just become one of the pastors at a church in Wenatchee, and I wanted to attend registration at the local Christian school. The only person I knew in the whole valley was Gene Roemer, the history teacher at the school. So I sat next to him, saying hi to all the students and parents who checked in at his table.

Shortly after I arrived, a 12-year-old boy came bouncing up to the table, looked at Gene, and said, "Hi, Dad."

I looked at Gene and said, "I didn't know you had a son!"

"I don't," he said. "This isn't a boy—it's a girl, and she's a senior in high school."

Meghan looked devastated that I thought she was a boy, but she shook it off and told me that it happened all the time.

Soon after I met her, I started to hear Meghan's story. When she was 9 years old, the police came into her home, arrested her mother and father, and separated the children into foster care. Evidently there had been some sort of organized ring of adults who had been abusing children, and Meghan was a witness for the prosecution.

The town of Wenatchee was split as to whether the people being accused of these heinous crimes were guilty or if there was a witch hunt to indict innocent people. The result was torturous to little Meghan. She was being picked on at school every day. Every day she would come home in tears, begging her foster mom not to make her go back to school the next day.

Finally, in an act of desperation, Meghan's foster family approached Cascade Christian Academy and enrolled her.

It was during Meghan's senior year that Meghan sat me down for a serious talk. She said, "This school and this church are family to me, and I want this to be a part of my family from now on. Would you baptize me? I want to be a part of this church and school family for the rest of my life."

It was my privilege to study Scripture with Meghan and watch her develop an absolutely precious relationship with her Creator. And it was also my privilege to walk out into the ocean at Rosario Beach near Anacortes, Washington, on a school-sponsored spiritual retreat and baptize her in front of her school family.

It wasn't long after that that Meghan started spending more and more time with Wendy, Cole, and me. I don't recall ever inviting her over—she'd just show up and stay for a few days at a time.

While in our home, Meghan began to share her life story with me, and it was during that time that she began to worm her way into the heart and life of our family.

Meghan moved into our home. Again, I don't remember inviting her— she just showed up with her stuff one day. Actually, she went behind my back and had my wife convinced that she needed to come live with us. My wife is such a softy.

It wasn't long after she moved in that she sat Wendy and me down and told us that she wanted to start calling us "Mom and Dad."

I felt pretty uncomfortable with that, and I told her so. She said, "I guess it doesn't matter to me if you feel uncomfortable about that, because that's what I'm calling you now."

While she lived with us, she became the daughter we never had. She shared her deepest joys, fears, hopes, dreams, and frustrations with us. She cheated at cards, rearranged her room 348 times, and gave the deepest shoulder and back rubs a person could experience without yelling in pain. She learned to drive, and we helped her purchase a car. She learned to work and got several jobs.

Meghan also became involved in her church in a way that would make most church-going adults hang their head in shame. She learned to love, and she shared that love with Wendy, Cole, and me. She made a pledge not to go down the road of substance abuse, tobacco, or alcohol. She figured life was too short and too precious to hand it over to something that could destroy her so fast.

Her diet consisted of candy, Life cereal, and uncooked Top Ramen. She loved oranges, but hated the taste of strawberries, peaches, and nectarines.

Every Sunday she'd mow the lawn, and every Sunday night she'd say, "Dad, you owe me 20 bucks." I'd tell her she missed a spot, and she would roll her eyes and hold her hand out.

Wendy, Cole, and I had plans with Meghan. We wanted to take her to Africa with us to go on safari and see the animals on the Masai Mara. We wanted to see her achieve in school and become the social worker she longed to become. We wanted to see her marry and have children of her own. We had plans.

Nothing crushed her like the times I expressed disappointment in a decision she made. Nothing made her glow like the times I told her I loved her and was proud of her.

Well, I couldn't love her or be more proud of the actions she took on her last Sabbath afternoon.

Meghan and a large group of youth were sitting alongside a river in the sun. Some people were swimming, while some were sitting and playing guitars. It was a perfect afternoon for lounging and enjoying one another's company. Two of the girls in the group had dozed off on an air mattress and had drifted to a dangerous end of the swimming hole toward some rapids that led to a torrential part of the river. Some men on the adjacent bank yelled a warning. That's when Meghan jumped to her feet and started running down the beach with the obvious intent to dive in and save the two young women.

Jesus said, "Greater love hath no man than this, that a man lay down his life for his friends."

When we went to the river this week, I found a rock that was stained with Meghan's blood. As I stood and looked at it, something dawned on me. Meghan and Jesus have something in common. Both of them spilled their blood in an attempt to save someone they loved and cared about.

The last time I saw Meghan was when she dropped me at the airport on Thursday night before the weekend she gave her life. We stood at the side of the car, and she hugged me tight and said, "I love you, Dad."

I said, "I love you, too."

The next time I see Meghan will be at the resurrection. She'll run to me and say, "I love you, Dad."

I'll hug her and say, "I love you, too."

We're so proud of her, and we miss her dearly. It just makes me all the more eager for Jesus to return, because resurrection morning is going to be a great reunion for me and my family.

Father, help me to be the kind of person who will love people so much that I will be willing to lay down my life for a friend. Thank You for laying down Your life for me. Amen.

CARROTS ALL GONE

"I am astonished that you are so quickly deserting the one who called you by the grace of Christ and are turning to a different gospel—which is really no gospel at all."
Galatians 1:6, 7.

In 1967 my family moved into the neighborhood I would live in until I graduated from high school. It was great because everybody knew everybody and almost everybody liked everybody. The exception to that rule was the person who lived right next to us. My mom and dad really liked Georgie, but she didn't like (or at least it didn't seem like she liked) kids.

Georgie was an eccentric middle-aged woman who liked things just so in her life. One part of her life that she liked just so was her garden. She had a big beautiful garden in her backyard with all kinds of vegetables in it. And every time we had a ball fly over the fence and into her garden, we knew we had to be careful to sneak over the fence and retrieve it, because if Georgie caught us, the screamfest would begin.

Georgie could scream better than any adult I've ever met. She'd threaten to call our parents, beat us with a paddle, or shoot us with her BB gun if we ever went near her precious garden again.

We didn't like Georgie very much.

One summer night all of my friends and I were sleeping in my neighbor's tree house. We had eaten all our junk food, told all the jokes we could remember, and were planning our next bit of fun when Tim said, "I'm still kind of hungry." The echoes around the little tree house acknowledged that none of our 10-year-old stomachs were quite full yet. It got quiet again. Tim continued, "You know what sounds really good? Fresh carrots. Don't fresh carrots sound good to you guys?"

Well, not really. I mean, I like carrots as much as the next guy, but I would rather have another bag of popcorn or another candy bar.

Then Tim got a little maniacal grin on his face. He said, "Hey, I know where we could get some fresh carrots. Georgie has a bunch of them growing in her garden!"

The whole tree house exploded with excitement. Thoughts of camouflaged

10-year-olds sneaking over the fence into enemy territory to steal buried treasure flooded our minds.

Then Tim took it one step further. "And I've got some replacement carrots so that Georgie won't get too mad at us!"

Sure enough, Tim had thought of this ahead of time. At the bottom of the fire pole buried in the sawdust by the shed was a bag of Playskool plastic carrots.

As quietly as we could, we sneaked over the fence and into Georgie's backyard. Tim had a flashlight and shone it on the carrots at the end of her garden. As each of us pulled two big beautiful carrots out of the ground, Tim replaced them with two of his little sister's plastic carrots, until there was a perfect little row of plastic carrots left for Georgie to discover in her garden.

The next morning we were shattered out of a deep sleep with a bloodcurdling scream. Georgie had come out to her garden to pick some raspberries for breakfast when she discovered our little prank.

Needless to say, we weren't allowed to sleep in the tree house for weeks after the trail of evidence led Georgie to my friends and me.

As evidenced by the great carrot debacle, there is nothing as good as the real thing. Plastic carrots aren't nearly as good in a salad as real carrots. Georgie was furious because the real thing was replaced by a fake.

In the Epistle to the Galatians, the apostle Paul comes off as quite upset because the church in Galatia was replacing the real gospel of Jesus Christ with a fake one. Somebody had come along and convinced the people in that church that they could somehow do something to their bodies that would make God love and accept them.

Paul realized and wrote to the Galatians that there is nothing you can do to earn God's love or His gift of salvation. Nothing fake about that!

Father, help me to live an authentic life and to settle only for a REAL life in You. Help me to identify cheap imitations that will lead me down the wrong path in life. Amen.

NEVER PLAY WOLF

"'For I know the plans I have for you,' declares the Lord, 'plans to prosper you and not to harm you, plans to give you hope and a future.'"
Jeremiah 29:11.

One of the most thrilling backpacking trips I've ever been on was to a place in British Columbia called the Rainbow Range. Each year we'd take our students from the little high school in Bella Coola on this wonderful hike, and each year we were thrilled by the views. At the trailhead our principal decided that I would take the lead and wait for the group at Lake M. That's right, many of the lakes above the tree line on the Rainbow Range are named after the letters in the alphabet.

Our plan was to take our kids to Lake M, camp overnight, take them to Octopus Lake (below the tree line), and hike out to the trailhead again. One of the best things about God is that our plans don't necessarily have anything to do with His plans.

On the way up the hill on our first day, I was feeling extra spry, and without realizing it, I jaunted up ahead of the group, creating quite a distance between us. When I finally realized that I was leaving my group in the dust, I stopped, turned around, and waited. I was swigging water from my water bottle as Tye, Albert, and Elwood came rumbling up the hill.

As Tye looked up, he froze and put his arms out to stop Albert and Elwood behind him. He looked at me with wide eyes and whispered a barely audible, "Turn around and look behind you! *Shhhhhhh!*"

I slowly turned around, and to my surprise, standing not 30 feet away from me, was the largest bull moose I'd ever seen. He must have been standing there the whole time I was waiting. I tend to hike with my head down (not a great way to catch all the action around me), so I just hadn't seen him.

He just stood there, watching me, not moving a muscle. I slowly put my pack down and slid my camera out of my side pocket. Slowly Albert, Tye, and Elwood inched up to where I was, and all four of us started snapping pictures as fast as we could.

The noise of the cameras must have convinced the moose to move on, and he gracefully rumbled through the brush and out of our sight. The four of us were jumping up and down and high-fiving each other as the rest of the group started to catch up. They quickly gathered around to hear our story. What a magnificent sight it was to see a huge bull moose that close!

After we all settled down and started hiking again, my lead once again grew as we traversed over one hill after another. We were now quite above the tree line, winding our way over the ridges looking for Lake M. Finally, I saw Lake M in the distance and started to make my way down the hill. About halfway down I found a little deer trail that I followed (head down to make sure I didn't lose my footing) as I made my way to our camp.

"Mr. Witas!"

I barely heard the call. Tye was yelling my name from the side of the little mountain we were hiking down. He had a clear vision of me because we were above the tree line. I turned around and gestured with my hands. Tye, Albert, and Elwood were about 300 yards behind me, and they were gesturing wildly for me to turn around and look behind me again.

I thought, *Wow, two moose (or is that mooses?) in one day. How lucky can a guy get?* But it wasn't a moose. It was a wolf. A big wolf. And it was about half the length of a basketball court away from me. And it was sitting in the middle of my deer trail staring at me like I was prime rib.

Wolves scare me more than moose do. I don't know why. Maybe it's because my mom never read me a story about Little Red Riding Hood and the Big Bad Moose. Nor had I ever read a story about a moose huffing and puffing and blowing a pig's house down. This was a wolf. A big wolf. With big teeth in its head. Looking at me.

I slowly lowered my pack and took out a small Swiss Army knife (the blade on the knife was broken, so I pulled my corkscrew out for protection). The wolf didn't move. I didn't know what to do. The guys behind me were getting closer and taking pictures now.

In a moment of sheer stupidity I decided to try to scare the wolf away so that the kids on our trip would be safe. I made a sudden move toward the wolf, clapped my hands, and yelled, "Hey!"

Instead of running, the wolf started to act as a dog acts when a person plays with it in the front yard. He started to jump around and then crouch and hold his position. I'd advance toward him again, and he'd jump and whirl around and crouch down again, wagging his tail.

One of the guys behind me yelled, "He's playing with you, Mr. Witas!"

This little game went on for three or four minutes until we all heard what sounded like thunder on the hill above us. As we looked up (the backpackers and the wolf), we saw a huge herd of elk running across the hill. The wolf looked at me, then looked at the herd. And then he made a quick decision. He ran full tilt over the hill after the elk.

What an experience! The guys and I hiked up to the top of the hill, took our lunches out, and started to eat. We just sat there not really saying anything for a while. Then Albert (not known for his eloquence) said, "Do you think God smiled this morning when He thought all this up for us?"

Great question. Yes, I think He did. God's plans for us are more than just for school, a career, or a boyfriend/girlfriend. His plans are more than where we are born and how and where we will die. He has daily plans for us! He surrounds us each day with opportunities to experience His smile on our lives as we live out our everyday lives as His children.

Father God, thank You for planning wonderful surprises in my life. Open my eyes to see the wonder that You provide me each day. Amen.

SPRING HARES AND FROG HUNTERS

*"Do not take revenge, my friends, but leave room for God's wrath, for it is written:
'It is mine to avenge; I will repay,' says the Lord."*
Romans 12:19.

I've taken six mission groups to Kenya, and each time has left me with memories that have made it the most enchanting and enjoyable short-term mission place I've ever visited. The Masai people are always appreciative. Our hosts, Andy and Debbie Aho, have built a special bit of heaven on the edge of an escarpment overlooking the vast expanse of the Masai Mara. It's simply the best place for missions I've had the privilege of visiting.

My last trip to Kenya was packed with wonderful memories. My father and I arrived a week early to see the animals of the Mara and relax on the porch of the bungalow overlooking the animal park. That trip left him with lifelong memories of leopards in trees, a cheetah on the hood of our vehicle, hippos grunting and snorting in the river, and lions roaring us to sleep at night. But my favorite memory of that particular trip actually happened a week later, after the rest of my mission group caught up with me.

It was a Tuesday night and one of our hosts, a handsome young man named Josh, took a handful of young people from our team on a "night safari." I put that in quotes because it was not as much a safari as a chase. Kenya is littered with spring hares, a kind of rabbit that looks like a small kangaroo. It was Josh's tradition that after dark he would take a group out, chase these little spring hares with his vehicle and a spotlight, catch a couple of them, sneak back into camp, and let them loose in the unsuspecting girls' tents after they were asleep.

After the group returned from their safari, they chose to release the spring hares in Clarissa and Jessica Fisher's tent. For some reason the girls didn't go on the night safari, and they were sound asleep when the spring hares were stealthily placed inside their tent.

The bloodcurdling shrieks that night could have awakened the dead.

The spring hares were so terrified by the girls' screams that they dug a hole through the side of the tent. And two girls woke up the next morning with one thing on their minds—revenge!

"Pastor Mark, Pastor Mark, will you go to the watering hole with us today?" The watering hole was the term used for the muddy water hole that was fed by an underground spring that (with the help of a generator and a water pump) fed water to the camp we were staying in.

"Why? Why would you want to go over there? There was a huge snake over there a couple of days ago," I replied.

They came closer with grins that only a sneaky person would wear. "We are going to get revenge on Josh!"

I've never been able to turn down the opportunity to get a cheap laugh from a good practical joke, so I asked what their plan was.

"We are going to catch a bunch of frogs and let them loose in his tent tonight! *Shhhh!* Will you help us?" they asked.

I was all in. They had managed to round up a butterfly net and a bucket, and before I knew it, we were standing at the side of the watering hole on a mission. First, Clarissa walked around the 8' x 10' hole of water with the net, searching intently for any sign of a frog in the muddy water. Sure enough, one hopped in and swam under the mucky water. She swiped the net at it, but missed. As she marched around we saw 10 to 15 frogs jump into the water. She missed all of them.

Then Jessica commandeered the net, and without a thought, she jumped into the waist-deep water and started swooping the net into the murky liquid, bringing up an empty net each time.

Clarissa and I started to laugh as we watched Jessica adapt a new tactic. In her best Elmer Fudd voice she looked at us and whispered, "*Shhhhh*. Be vewy, vewy quiet! We're hunting fwogs." Then she'd turn around and bury the net in the water, trying to catch the frogs by surprise. It still didn't work.

Then she switched tactics again. She told Clarissa and me that we needed to start thinking like a frog. "If I were a frog, where would I hide right now?" and "I think we need to think like frog psychologists."

It started to rain. Hard. Our little revenge trip became an exercise in futility. We ended up marching into camp soaked to the bone with an empty butterfly net and an empty bucket. And to make matters worse, Josh was standing in the lodge area, dry, with a smile on his face. When we came in, he looked at the girls and said, "Find any frogs?" How humiliating! The sweet taste of revenge would have to wait till another day.

This story, of course, is the story of a game between friends. Not too serious, no big deal. Unfortunately, some people take revenge to a different level.

"Vengeance." "Revenge." "Payback." These words conjure up feelings of anger and regret. And, truth be told, those words usually bring about actions that are often not worth your effort because the reward of feeling like you've accomplished something rarely comes with revenge.

Remember, God takes care of His children. When you exact revenge, you are taking God's place and doing His work without His permission to do so.

The opposite of revenge is forgiveness. In fact, the Bible says, "If you forgive men when they sin against you, your heavenly Father will also forgive you. But if you do not forgive men their sins, your Father will not forgive your sins" (Matt. 6:14, 15).

Scary words for a person filled with thoughts of revenge. I've heard it said that "not forgiving someone when they wrong you is like trying to kill the rats in your house by drinking rat poison."

Let God be God. He promises that in the end, justice will be done. And do yourself a favor, learn to forgive and let sleeping frogs lie.

Father in heaven, lead me to the place in my life where I can let go of my past and forgive the people who have harmed me, even if they aren't sorry for what they've done. I know this can take some time, so please be patient with me. Help me to learn to do things Your way, because Your way is the best way. Amen.

GEO RAFTER

"You also must be ready, because the Son of Man will come at an hour when you do not expect him."
Luke 12:40.

The most frustrating thing about the unexpected is that it's so . . . unexpected. Most people like to know what's going on before it happens. It gives them the security of having some sort of expectation so that they can in some small way control their future. We like to have that small measure of comfort to know just enough to plan.

That's why some people get frustrated with Jesus' remark in Matthew 24: "No one knows the day or the hour [of the Second Coming] not even Me!" In fact, not only do we not know when it's going to happen, but when it does come we aren't even going to expect it! Complete surprise. Like a thief in the night. So what's a Christian to do?

According to Scripture, be ready.

It was May 2007 when the geocaching group from Seattle called and said they wanted to go white-water rafting and geocaching down the Wenatchee River. I told them no. The river was at flood stage and had more water going down it than ever recorded. It was running at 20,000 CFS (cubic feet per second). That meant that some of the rapids would be 16 feet high and very violent. Definitely not for a bunch of rookie rafting geochachers.

As it turned out, the geocachers convinced my partner and me that they were fine with the risk and really wanted to come that weekend. We had them all sign a waver before we got on the water that basically said, "If you die during this trip, we aren't liable," and off we went.

The river was huge (it was running about 16,000 CFS that day), and as we started out, we were having a great time hitting big waves and getting wet in the spring sun. And then it happened. Just before a fun little pullout called Arco Eddie, my raft hit a rapid a little sideways and before we could blink, the raft was upside down and everyone was in the river . . . at flood stage. I had guided down that river more than 100 times and never flipped a raft. Why did it have to happen during flood stage with a bunch of rookies?

In no time at all the other guides in our group had their rafts mobilized to take care of the problem. Throw lines were in the water, people were being rescued, and I was on the top (bottom, technically) of our raft grabbing the flip lines to get us right-side up. In a matter of minutes everyone was in the raft—shaken—but safe.

Why? Why was this potentially life-threatening emergency handled so smoothly with such a good outcome? Planning and practice.

Each year before we take groups out on a white-water adventure, our staff sits down and plans for the worst. We plan and we practice. We prepare for what's going to happen just in case it does. As we tell all our groups, we don't expect the raft to flip, but if it does, we have a plan and everyone will be OK.

I think that's what the Bible teaches us about the end of time. We don't know when it is going to happen. We have some clues and things that Jesus and the apostles and prophets have told us to look for to give us a little heads-up, but all in all, we don't have a clue when Jesus is going to come back.

So what's a Christian to do? Be prepared every day like it could be today. Every day, take some time to be right with God. Every day, practice your faith to make you stronger for the rocky times ahead. And every day, be ready, because one day, someday, will be our last day on this earth. Whether we get the privilege of seeing our Savior come for us, or whether we end up breathing our last breath on this earth, we can be ready. Maranatha. Come quickly, Lord Jesus!

Father, live in me. Breathe in me so that I am ready for anything this life dishes out. I want to be ready every day for whatever You have in store for me. And if this is my last day on earth, I am not afraid, because I am living in You. Amen.

STUPID DOCTORS

"Do not be deceived: God cannot be mocked. A man reaps what he sows."
Galatians 6:7.

Have you ever known people who get themselves in all kinds of trouble and then blame everyone around them for the trouble they received? It's like the stories I've read in the newspaper about a criminal who is burglarizing a home. While they are robbing someone's personal property, they slip and fall on the linoleum in the kitchen and sue the homeowners for having a slippery floor. *Are you kidding me?*

What has happened to our society? We've raised a generation who refuses to look at themselves in the mirror and admit that whatever bind they are in is their fault. Self-created. They refuse to see what an old preacher friend of mine used to say, "If you gonna lie down with da dogs, you gonna get da fleas!"

My stepfather was this kind of guy. He spent 18 years in prison before my mom met and married him. His whole life was a big excuse about how everyone else was at fault for his lot in life. If he got pulled over and got a ticket, the police officer was picking on him. If he had a collection agency after him for unpaid bills, the people he owed money were "stupid." When he refused to go to church with my mom, he said, "All those people in that stupid church are just too judgmental." How ironic.

Don, my stepfather, smoked like a chimney. I'm not sure how many cigarettes he smoked every day, but it was a lot. My aunts and uncles would get him cartons of cigarettes for Christmas. I know, it sounds weird, but it's true. Don smoked a lot.

Don got throat cancer. He didn't work. He didn't have any money. He didn't have insurance. Even so, the good people at the University of Washington Medical Center took on his case. They cut the cancer out, gave him radiation, and basically cured him (physically).

After losing 80 pounds in the battle, Don finally got all his treatments done and was debt-free of the procedures through the generosity of charities and physicians. I asked him how he felt about being on the victorious side of cancer.

His answer almost knocked me to the ground. "Those stupid doctors gave me radiation, and now I can't taste my food very good. I should sue them."

I couldn't even respond. What an ingrate. What kind of person would bring something like that upon themselves, get bailed out of the situation, and be mad at and blame the people around him for the predicament?

But let's face it, we're all human. We all do it. We all do things that get us into trouble, and then we complain about suffering the consequences. It started with Adam and Eve. Eve blamed the snake, and Adam blamed Eve and God. And ever since the garden, people have avoided taking responsibility for their own actions.

The Bible teaches us two things about this. First, as our text for today says, a man reaps what he sows. You smoke, you get cancer. You eat too much, you get fat. You speed, you get a ticket. You treat people poorly, they will treat you poorly. See the pattern? We reap what we sow. Call it karma, call it God's sense of humor, call it a natural law, call it whatever you want to, but most of the time we receive what we put out.

Second, there is a way to take responsibility for our actions that is both responsible and healing—it's called confession. First John 1:9 says, "If we confess our sins, he is faithful and just and will forgive us our sins and purify us from all unrighteousness."

In other words, if we take responsibility for our actions before God and the people around us, not only will we be forgiven of the ridiculous situations we find ourselves in, but He will absolve us of it and treat us as though we never acted stupid in the first place.

Aren't you glad that we have a God who treats us like this? Wouldn't it be nice if more Christians would take responsibility for their own actions and confess their sins instead of blaming everyone around them for their situations?

Father, give me the wisdom and the courage to admit when I'm wrong. Keep me from blaming anyone but myself for the trouble I get myself in. Make me a person of integrity. Amen.

BLINDED BY THE LIGHT

"There is a way that seems right to a man, but in the end it leads to death."
Proverbs 14:12.

Saul found a niche in the church. His claim to fame was his ability to find and root out any heresy that might arise in the midst of God's people. He would sniff it out like a bloodhound after a criminal. And he was good at it.

It was during his rise to fame that Saul started to hear about another up-and-coming Rabbi named Jesus. This Jesus sounded like any number of other false prophets who popped up in Palestine from time to time—lots of followers, fake healings, good storyteller. So the news of this Jesus' death didn't come as a surprise to Saul. After all, eventually the charlatans were all discovered and given their just reward—death.

What was disturbing to Saul was that all the fuss about Jesus didn't go away after He died. In fact, just the opposite was happening. He had a growing group of disciples who were actually claiming that He had risen from the dead, and if that weren't enough, they were now claiming that this Jesus had ascended to heaven and was actually sitting in judgment over the earth next to the right hand of Yahweh Himself!

Saul had heard all kinds of blasphemy, but never had he seen this kind of blasphemy take off and threaten the church like this. He was curious, and he wanted to know more about this growing cult. So he traveled to Jerusalem to offer his services.

When he got there, Saul found the city in a stir. This cult of strange believers had stirred things up quite a bit, and now they were numbering in the thousands. His work was going to be a lot tougher than he had thought. He was greeted warmly by Gamaliel (his university professor) that day and was invited to observe a trial that was going to take place in the Sanhedrin in just a short time.

They had arrested one of the cult members named Stephen. This Stephen was an elected leader of this new cult, and he needed to be investigated.

Gamaliel seemed to be more curious than angry at what these "Christians" were teaching.

The next day, at the trial, Saul almost had to laugh as he saw the man Stephen brought before them. He seemed like a simple sort, not educated to the degree that any of the men sitting in judgment had been. In fact, Saul wondered if the poor sap knew how to read at all. He was probably a common laborer, maybe a fisherman. Regardless, his intellect would be no match for the men of the Sanhedrin.

The trial started, and Stephen remained silent for the first while. Then, when given a chance to speak, Stephen shocked Saul and the crowd with a very thorough recitation of the history of the Jewish people. Saul was actually kind of impressed.

But then Stephen's speech took an unexpected and ugly turn. This horrible little cult member, this freak of a warped theology, actually tried to plug Holy Scripture into his belief system to support this nonsensical Messiah he was talking about.

The words he spoke were so horrible, so out of bounds, so offensive to God, that the whole assembly rose as one, grabbed Stephen, and dragged him from that place toward a place outside the city reserved for the worst kind of blasphemers. As they were dragging him, this delusional cult member started declaring that he was seeing this "Jesus" in heaven and that He was going to rule the world someday!

The men threw dirt up in the air and started yelling nonsense themselves just to drown out the horrible blasphemies this man was saying.

Finally, they got to the place assigned to deal with the most dangerous spiritual poison. If only this man Stephen could know the Scriptures like he (Saul) did. But no, instead he had to read his belief system into the Bible and threaten God's remnant, and in so doing, forfeit his own life.

One by one the stones started raining on him. The poor sap actually looked at peace as that last stone hit the side of his head with a thundering *crack*! Finally the man slumped over—dead. It was finished. And Saul, for one, had found his calling. God wanted him to seek out the rest of the leadership of this cult and bring them to the same fate.

Sometimes—not all the time, but sometimes—we can get so wrapped up in our opinions, our prescriptions, and our certainty of what God's will is, even backing up our opinions with the Bible itself, that we can blind ourselves to the reality of God's will in our lives or in the lives of others.

It happened all the time in the Bible:

- King Saul and David's father and brothers would have never picked David to defeat Goliath.
- The disciples, "doing the will of Jesus," tried to protect Him from children. Jesus rebuked them and embraced the children.
- Judas tried to push Jesus into the most logical of all conclusions about His reason for being on earth. He was going to be the King of the Jews and free Israel from the Romans, right?
- The disciples and the "good people" of the world tried to protect Jesus from Zacchaeus.
- Eve took a bite of the fruit so she could be just like God.

In each of these cases, people had things figured out. They "knew" the will of God. At least they thought they did. But in each case, God had a different plan. In some cases, certainly in Saul's, people had Scripture (or at least their understanding of it) to back up the reasons they did things the way they did.

But we forget that God sometimes uses unconventional means to do great things on this earth:

- He placed a coin in a fish's mouth to pay the Temple tax.
- He parted the Red Sea.
- He chose a healed demoniac to witness and bring 10 cities to Jesus.
- He took down a thousand of His enemies with a dumb ox and the jawbone of a donkey.
- He filled a room with fire and wind, sending 120 believers into the streets to kick-start His new church.
- He chooses fallen, broken people—like you and me—to be His hands and feet in the world, even though we aren't exactly superstars for the gospel.

Sometimes we need to step back from our opinions, step back from what we absolutely know about a subject or about a person, or what we think God's will is, and let God be God.

Saul started to catch and execute the leaders of the cult one by one. But it was frustrating. Each time he'd kill one, it seemed as though 10 more would pop up.

And then one day, as Saul was traveling with his posse into Damascus, something unexpected happened. The combination of the blinding brightness and the loud thunderclap was bewildering, unexplainable, and certainly disorienting. Had he been struck by lightning? Maybe this was it. Maybe this was the time God had chosen for him to die.

And then he heard the voice. "Saul, Saul, why are you persecuting Me?" No. NO! It couldn't be. Not according to everything he had studied. Not according to everything he knew to be true!

"Who are you, Lord?"

"I'm Jesus. I'm alive. And now it's time for you to stop killing My people. In fact, I have chosen you to be on My side. The life you have lived up to now is going to change. You will no longer live for prestige; you will no longer read Scripture and apply it as you see fit. I'm going to give you a new paradigm, a new way of thinking. Now go and wait in the city, and I'll send someone to open your eyes, both physically and spiritually."

"Oh, and Saul?"

"Yes, Lord?"

"From now on, you're going to have a new name. Your new name will be Paul."

"Yes, Lord."

How is it that a man such as Saul could study the Scriptures so thoroughly and still get it wrong? How could a man such as Saul spend that many hours in prayer and still have the wrong idea about who God is and what He expects?

Here's my take on the whole story: If the zeal you have for your religion causes you to want to do harm to another person, or causes you to want to coerce or force someone to believe like you do or act like you think they ought to act, step back and take a breath. Reexamine your relationship with Jesus. Look at how He related to people and did things while He was here on earth.

He didn't call people names. He didn't coerce people. He didn't use force to have anyone follow Him or act correctly. The only people He yelled at were religious people who used coercion, manipulation, and force to get people to act like they thought they should act. No, He invited them into His presence, ministered to their needs, and loved them.

God had to knock Saul off a horse to get his attention. What does He have to do to get your attention?

Jesus, I want You to tell me where my heart is hard, where my opinions are wrong, and where my life needs to change. And if I've settled on an opinion that isn't Your will, knock me off my horse and get my attention, because I want to do Your will. Amen.

PANTS ON FIRE!

"You belong to your father, the devil, and you want to carry out your father's desire.
He was a murderer from the beginning, not holding to the truth,
for there is no truth in him. When he lies, he speaks his native language,
for he is a liar and the father of lies."
John 8:44.

The devil is a liar. I think there are three specific lies the devil tells that have done the most harm to the people I love in my family and in God's church. Here they are (the lies, not the people!):

Lie Number One: God could never love someone like you.

"Oh, Pastor, you don't know what I've done. And for some reason, Pastor, I can't conquer this one sin in my life. God could never love someone like me."

Really? How can a person respond to such a hellish whopper? Look at Romans 8:35-39. God clearly refutes this lie: "Who shall separate us from the love of Christ? Shall trouble or hardship or persecution or famine or nakedness or danger or sword? As it is written: 'For your sake we face death all day long; we are considered as sheep to be slaughtered.' No, in all these things we are more than conquerors through him who loved us. For I am convinced that neither death nor life, neither angels nor demons, neither the present nor the future, nor any powers, neither height nor depth, nor anything else in all creation, will be able to separate us from the love of God that is in Christ Jesus our Lord."

This powerful text should shatter that lie of the devil. God loves you. He loves you with an everlasting, unquenchable love. To believe anything else is to believe a lie.

Lie Number Two: Your behavior doesn't matter. All that matters is that God loves you.

This lie has rationalized more blatant disobedience to God's Word than any other lie in the church. I've seen couples rationalize their physical behavior before marriage with this one, "All that matters is that we love each other and that God loves us."

Mixed with God's unquenchable love for us is God's desire for us to be obedient to His Word. He wants us to embrace the truth of His love *and* live that truth.

Jesus said it a few different ways, but the most powerful and to the point was in John 14: "If you love Me, keep My commandments."

Lie number two stands on the premise that it doesn't matter what you do, because God loves you. The truth is that *it does matter what you do,* and *God loves you.*

Lie Number Three: God may not be able to save me because I'm such a sinner.

This lie has done as much to damage the church of Christ as any because the more we buy into this lie, the less effective we become in sharing the gospel. After all, if we aren't sure about our salvation—our ultimate destination, if you will—then how could the gospel be *good news?*

We've paraphrased John 3:16 so that it reads, "For God so loved the world that He gave His only Son, that whoever believes in Him, *maybe might not* perish, but *possibly might have a stab at* eternal life *if he gets lucky and God's in a good mood that day.*"

The devil is a liar! And this lie flies directly in the face of what Scripture teaches. Look at 1 John 5:13: "I write these things to you who believe in the name of the Son of God so that you may *know* that you have eternal life."

Romans 8:1 says that if you believe, there is no condemnation for you. Believers are saved. Period. End of discussion. Everything else is a lie that comes directly from the devil. No ifs, ands, or buts. If you are walking with the Lord, your eternity is secure.

So let's live in the truth and throw the devil's lies in the garbage, where they belong.

Jesus, give me the discernment to know the devil's lies. Help me to memorize the promises You have placed in Your Word and not believe what Satan tries to whisper in my ears about who I am. Help me to remember that I am a child of the King and that there is no condemnation for me. Amen.

HIT 'EM OVER THE HEAD WITH A STICK

"Wounds from a friend can be trusted, but an enemy multiplies kisses."
Proverbs 27:6.

OK, I'm big. As I've mentioned before, I'm six feet six, and I weigh 225 pounds. That's bigger than most people. I don't notice I'm bigger than most people until I see myself in pictures with "normal" people. And then I think, *Wow, I'm huge!*

Another time I realized I was big was while I was driving in traffic just north of Seattle. I had mistakenly cut a car off behind me. I know this because the offended driver was honking at me and showing me the universal signal for displeasure. I've always enjoyed it when people do that, so I waved and smiled as the angry man raced by me on the wrong side of the road. This made him angrier, so he cut in front of me, slammed on his brakes, got out of his car, and ran back to mine. He actually started banging on my window, saying, "Why don't you get out of the car and wave at me, mister?"

So I did. As I stood up, the man (who stood about five feet nine and 150 pounds) looked way up at me and yelled, "Never mind!" He ran back to his car and raced off, never to be seen again. So I guess being big has its advantages.

But not so when I was young. When I was young, I was always the size of people four years older than I was. And that was a problem, because those were the people I seemed to hang around. One of those people moved into my neighborhood when I was 10 years old. His name was Gordon. He was in the eighth grade, and man, was Gordon cool!

He was 14, good-looking, athletic, and liked and listened to the coolest music. Everyone wanted to be like Gordon. Everyone wanted Gordon to pick them for his team. The problem was that Gordon loved to tease. And my life was made wonderful or horrible depending on whom Gordon's target for teasing was on any given day.

Most days Gordon would pick on Kenny Snart. (I mean, come on, with a last name like Snart you deserve to be picked on a little, right?) And sometimes Gordon would pick on Tim Cook or Mike Palmer. On those days I'd stand beside Gordon and laugh while he made my other friends miserable. But then there were the days he'd turn his teasing toward me.

I don't know why I let him get to me, but I did. He'd take my watch and not give it back. He'd take my shoe and not give it back. He'd threaten me with bodily harm, although I don't recall him ever physically hurting me. I'd end up running home with one shoe and no watch, and I'd start crying when I got into the house, "Dad, Gordon is picking on me! Go and tell him to give me my shoe back!"

My dad's suggestion always infuriated me. Not because it was a bad suggestion (it really was), but because I knew if I actually carried it out, Gordon would end my life. Dad would look up from his newspaper and say, "Hit him over the head with a stick."

Hit him over the head with a stick? How ridiculous is that? And to make matters worse, while I'd be crying to my dad about it, I'd see Gordon and Kenny Snart peeking through my front window and laughing at me.

Well, as it turned out, one day I'd had enough. Gordon had my watch, and he wouldn't give it back. He was holding it up so that I couldn't reach it, mocking me every time I'd try to grab it.

I ran home and started crying to Dad about it. Finally Dad put down his paper and said, "Hit him over the head with a stick."

I was so mad I ran out of the house and down the street to where Gordon and Snart were standing, laughing at me.

I looked around for a stick. There was no stick. So I closed my eyes, swung my fist as hard as I could, and punched Gordon in the stomach.

My sudden act of aggression caught Gordon by surprise, and he dropped the watch. I picked it up and ran for my life back to the house. That was the last time Gordon picked on me. And we've been best friends since. As I'm writing this story, Gordon and his family just left our house after visiting for the weekend. That's right, 36 years later we are still great friends.

As our text for the day suggests: "Wounds from a friend can be trusted." I didn't hit Gordon because I didn't like him. I hit him because I knew—somewhere deep in my 10-year-old psyche—that he needed to be hit so that we could be friends and not have these little conflicts anymore.

I've had plenty of friendships in which I needed to be hit—not by a fist, but by hard words. I've had friends have to tell me that I was acting inappropriately or that I had hurt them by something I did or said. But wounds from a friend can be trusted.

When someone who loves you tells you something about yourself that hurts, listen to them. Don't knee-jerk a sarcastic answer or walk away offended. Listen to what they are saying and evaluate it for what it is—a wound from a friend—because hard words spoken in love may be just what you need to hear to make you a little bit more like Jesus.

Dear God, please help me to be self-aware enough to listen to constructive criticism, so that I can be a better person and act more like Jesus. Help me to be the kind of friend You want me to be to those around me. Amen.

SMELLS LIKE SOMETHING'S DEAD

"For you created my inmost being; you knit me together in my mother's womb."
Psalm 139:13.

One of the strangest dates I've ever been on was with a wonderful girl who eventually became my wife. When I called her and asked her out, she told me that she would love to do something with me (an appropriate answer, if I do say so myself), but that she was going to be a little late getting to her place. She told me where she hid the key to her apartment (under the front mat), and to let myself in and wait for her if she was delayed longer than she expected.

When I reached her place, she wasn't there, so I let myself in. I sat on the couch in her living room and waited. And waited—I hate waiting. I got bored. So I did what no decent person should do: I started snooping. I looked through the photo albums in her living room. I looked in her refrigerator and some of her kitchen drawers. I looked in her bathroom. (Yes, I peeked in the medicine cabinet. I was still growing in Jesus.)

As I came out of her bathroom I was facing a door that was obviously a guest bedroom. I turned the handle of the door and started to open it. About a foot in, the door stopped. It had hit something so that it couldn't open anymore.

I was curious. So I tried again. It was still stuck. So I maneuvered my head so that I could see what was blocking the door. As I did, I couldn't believe what I was seeing. There was a mound of clothing that looked similar in size to Mount Everest. It was laundry. Dirty laundry.

Just as I pulled my head out of the doorway, I heard the front doorknob jiggling. I raced into the living room, sat on the couch, and picked up a magazine. Wendy came in and apologized for being late. She dropped some things on her kitchen table, and said, "So, what are we going to do tonight?"

I hemmed and hawed and said, "If you want, we can pick up a couple of sandwiches to go and do some laundry." (Wendy didn't have a washer and dryer in her apartment; she had to do her laundry at a Laundromat.)

She looked puzzled for a split second and then turned red with embarrassment. "You looked in the room, didn't you?"

I admitted my sin, "Yup. Sorry. I'll help if you want to do some laundry."

As we piled laundry into garbage bags, Wendy explained to me that she had two older sisters who loved to shop and would give Wendy all their old clothes. She loved it because her sisters had good taste and she got free clothes.

We piled the mound of laundry in the back of my truck, stopped and picked up a couple of sandwiches, and drove to the Laundromat.

We were the only people there besides a mother with several little children. Without separating any of the colors or types of fabric, Wendy started shoving dirty clothes into washers and turning them on.

We sat and talked until all the washers started to buzz. I watched in amazement as the woman I would one day marry heaped loads of wet laundry (again, without sorting it) into huge industrial dryers and set them on "bake."

Another hour went by, and the dryer buzzers all went off. Wendy heaped the fresh, clean laundry onto a big table in the middle of the room and we started to sort and fold. As we sorted and folded, two things started to happen that got my attention. First, a little boy from the family in the Laundromat started running under my legs, laughing and looking up at me. Second, I started to smell something offensive, slightly at first, but stronger as time went on.

I assumed that the little boy had deposited an accident in his pants, and tried to ignore the smell at first. But as we sorted the laundry, the smell got so strong that I thought I was going to gag. Finally I picked the little kid up and gave him a sniff. He was as clean as a whistle; it wasn't him.

I looked at Wendy, scrunching my nose. "Do you smell that?"

"Yes! Is that you?" she asked.

"No. I thought it was you," I retorted.

Offended by the insinuation, Wendy looked at me and said, "Well, it's not me!"

As we continued to sort and fold, the smell got more and more sour until I heard a whimper and saw a tear form in Wendy's eye. She was looking into the pile of laundry as though she was seeing a ghost.

Finally she reached into the pile and pulled out a little tiny sweater. It looked like it could fit a small stuffed animal of some kind. Wendy started to cry.

"What is that?" I asked.

"It's a sweater that my dad bought me for Christmas. It was really expensive. And I fried it." Wendy sobbed. She put it up to her nose and sniffed, "And, ooooooh, it smells like a dead animal. I don't think I was supposed to wash or dry it."

Sure enough, it was the source of our mystery odor. We took it over to the garbage can and gave it a proper burial. I decided that if we were to get married, I'd do my own laundry.

You are unique. I am unique. God made us just like He wanted us. He wired us to be just who we are with all our little quirks and oddities. Like snowflakes, no two of us are alike.

So what would happen if a church were to teach or preach that everyone should worship God in the same way, everyone should praise God in the same way, and everyone should experience their walk with God in the same way? I'll tell you what would happen. You'd end up with a bunch of ex-church members.

In the same way that our laundry needs to be sorted, some receiving different care than others, so each individual has their own path to God in Jesus Christ. Not everyone is going to respond to every sermon, every song, every appeal in the same way.

If Christians were laundry, some of us would be fine in the normal cycle, some of us would need the gentle cycle, others would need to be gently hand washed, and yes, some of us could be taken down to the creek and beat with rocks . . . at least some of the people I go to church with could.

Dear Jesus, help me to see people as You see them. Help me to realize that not everyone is led down the same path I am and that the things they like or don't like may have little to do with right or wrong but a lot to do with the path You have led them down. Help me to realize that my job is to accept people and love them, not to judge them. Amen.

WATCH OUT FOR THAT HORSE!

"Therefore put on the full armor of God, so that when the day of evil comes, you may be able to stand your ground, and after you have done everything, to stand."
Ephesians 6:13, TNIV.

Protection. My thesaurus lists the following words as synonyms for protection: "armor," "cover," "defense," "insurance," "precaution," "preservation," "safety," and "security."

I've come to realize that we spend our whole lives trying to protect ourselves and those we love, oftentimes purchasing products that help us accomplish that goal. Let me share an illustration.

A few years ago my wife and I spent Christmas with her parents in a little town on the coast of British Columbia. It was about a 13-hour drive from Seattle, where we lived, and with that drive came about a 300-mile trek from Williams Lake to Bella Coola, which was our destination. Our drive there was pleasant, and we made it in relatively good time. But our drive back was fraught with complications. First of all, we almost hit a deer only an hour into our journey. Just as we stopped shaking from that experience, we nearly hit a little red fox that seemed to be limping in the middle of the road.

About three hours later, as we came around a snowy corner in the middle of the night, I saw two Belgian logging horses in the middle of the road. I was doing about 55 miles per hour and thought that maybe I could sneak between them. Slamming on my brakes on a snowy road was out of the question.

As I maneuvered my vehicle to miss the two horses, one of them moved directly into my line of flight. There was a deadening thud, the sound of glass shattering, and then silence as the car came to rest in the snowbank on the side of the road.

For a second, I just sat there, unable to say anything. Then I looked over at Wendy to see if she was OK. The glass and the frame of the windshield were inches from her face, but she seemed to be fine. I had to force my door open to get out. I looked around and found that my car and the horse were about in the same condition—totaled.

I gathered my senses and looked back in the car as Wendy struggled to get out. She had glass in her hair from the back window shattering, and a scrape on the side of her forehead. Other than that, we were both OK.

It wasn't until we visited our dearly departed automobile at the car graveyard that we realized how close Wendy had actually come to death. The man at the body shop explained to us what would have happened if Wendy hadn't worn her seat belt. The impact of our collision sent a good part of the horse up onto the hood of our car, nearly sending him through our window. If Wendy hadn't been wearing her seat belt, she would have traveled through the windshield and met the horse head-on. And that likely (according to the body man and our insurance agent) would have killed her.

Car manufacturers put seat belts in cars for our protection. When we hear of a fatal car accident and find that the person who was killed wasn't wearing a seat belt, it's hard not to shake our heads and wonder what would possess a person to actually ride down a road at 50 miles per hour and not take advantage of this free protection offered them.

God is in the business of protecting His children. One of the primary tools He's given us is what the book of Ephesians calls the "armor of God."

"Therefore put on the full armor of God, so that when the day of evil comes, you may be able to stand your ground, and after you have done everything, to stand. Stand firm then, with the belt of truth buckled around your waist, with the breastplate of righteousness in place, and with your feet fitted with the readiness that comes from the gospel of peace. In addition to all this, take up the shield of faith, with which you can extinguish all the flaming arrows of the evil one. Take the helmet of salvation and the sword of the Spirit, which is the word of God. And pray in the Spirit on all occasions with all kinds of prayers and requests. With this in mind, be alert and always keep on praying for all the Lord's people" (Ephesians 6:13-18, TNIV).

It's my opinion that God's Word is a key component in fitting yourself with the armor of God. It seems to me that if you are rooted in God's Word and from it know what it means to live a great life, you will avoid doing some of the things that could take your armor off and make you vulnerable. God's Word is like life's little seat belt. Don't drive down the road without it!

Dear Jesus, thank You for being my fortress and my protection. Help me to realize how vulnerable I am when I walk outside of Your protection. Help me to prepare for the battle by arming myself with Your Word. Amen.

PROMISES, PROMISES

"Now the Lord said to Abram, 'Go from your country and your kindred and your father's house to the land that I will show you. I will make of you a great nation, and I will bless you, and make your name great, so that you will be a blessing. I will bless those who bless you, and the one who curses you I will curse; and in you all the families of the earth shall be blessed.' So Abram went, as the Lord had told him; and Lot went with him. Abram was seventy-five years old when he departed from Haran."
Genesis 12:1, NRSV.

One day God visited Abram with a very specific message and plan for his life. Talk about turning your world upside down!

So God told Abram to pack up his family and all of his belongings and move to an unknown land, and Abram, not knowing where he was going to end up, simply obeyed. I would say that this was an exhibition of huge faith. He just packed up and left. And that faith was rewarded as Abram pulled into Canaan. God again blessed him by saying "to your offspring I will give this land." What offspring?

Did you ever wonder why Abram brought Lot with him? I believe that when Abram was confronted with God's promise that he was going to become the father of many nations, Abram couldn't see how God could fulfill that promise in him. After all, he was 75 years old. I think Lot was plan B. As we continue in the story, you will see why I think that.

God had promised that Abram would be the father of many nations and that his offspring would inherit the land. Now at this point, he had only one wife, Sarai. And so far, in between the time Abram moved and settled in Canaan, Sarai showed no signs of pregnancy. The next thing we know about Abram is that he was on his way to Egypt because of a drought in Canaan. When he got into Egypt, Pharaoh saw Sarai and just about turned inside out with desire. She was either a real looker or a great political catch. When he approached Abram and asked about Sarai, Abram told a half-truth and let Pharaoh take her into his court to be his wife! When was the last time you saw a hero in a movie say, "Do what you want to the woman, but leave me alone!"

And what about the promise? God said, "I'll make a nation out of you."

How was God going to do that if Abram gave his wife away? God had to intervene and solve the problem. And before Abram knew it, he and Sarai were together again. I wonder what she said to Abram after they got back together. "Thanks a lot, honey; I almost helped the king of Egypt become a great nation!"

Obviously Abram didn't think Sarai was going to bear him any children, or he wouldn't have given her away so quickly. He must have been banking on the promise being fulfilled in some other way. Maybe Lot was going to be his heir. Or not.

Lot and his family couldn't get along with Abram and his family, and Lot moved to Sodom. So much for plan B.

Enter plan C. In Genesis 15 God came to Abram again to reaffirm His promise. Obviously Abram was wondering about God's ability to keep His promise, so he made another suggestion. He said, "God, what if I adopt my head slave, Eliezer of Damascus? He's a good guy. He can be my son. There, now that nice little promise You made me can be fulfilled."

God said, "No. Abram, come outside with Me. Look up at the stars. Can you count them?"

"No, Lord, there are too many."

"Neither will you be able to count your descendants. Abram, you are going to have a son. And that son is going to come from your own body." And the Bible says that Abram believed God this time . . . for a while.

But time kept marching on, and Sarai did not get pregnant. And the longer they waited, the more impatient Abram and Sarai became.

Enter plan D. Finally Sarai got so sick of waiting that she told Abram, "Listen, I'm not going into the tent with you anymore. Here, take my young maidservant as your wife; she can bear you a child."

Abram looked at Hagar and said, "OK!"

And Hagar had a son. And Sarai became bitter and jealous, a natural response to the unnatural act of having more than one spouse. And Abram's second wife was mistreated until she had to run away. And it was painful. The son Abram thought God had promised him couldn't even live with him. What kind of promise was that?

And God came to Abram again. He said, "Abram, don't you remember the covenant I made with you? I'm going to give you a son. And Sarai is going to bear that son."

Abram fell down on his face and laughed at God. "I'm sorry, Lord, but do You really think that a man of 100 years and a woman of 90 years are going to have a son?"

God said, "Abram, get a knife."

Have you ever wondered why God chose circumcision as a covenant for Israel? Here's your answer. God was saying, "Abram, you have trusted Me with many things. You have trusted Me enough to move to this foreign land. You have trusted Me with your wealth so much that you pay tithe to My priest in Salem, a guy named Melchizedek. But there is one thing, Abram, one part of you, that you haven't trusted Me with. And now I need a tithe of that, also."

I don't mean to be crass, but the covenant of circumcision had to happen because it was the only way that Abram was going to learn that he had to trust that God keeps His promises. The act of circumcision was a symbolic act that said, "Yes, God, I trust You even with this part of my life." I wish that circumcision could mean the same thing to so many men today.

I believe that it was this covenant that finally got to Abram. It was during this covenant that God changed Abram's name to Abraham, literally meaning, "I've already made you a father of many nations." It's a done deal. I've said it, you believe it, because it's going to happen.

Now look with me at one of the most powerful texts in the Bible. Check this language out.

"The Lord dealt with Sarah as he had said, and the Lord did for Sarah as he had promised. Sarah conceived and bore Abraham a son in his old age, at the time of which God had spoken to him" (Genesis 21:1, 2, NRSV).

Did you notice the language here? There is only one other place in the whole Bible where this kind of language is used. It's in the New Testament dealing with a young virgin named Mary, who was given another child of promise.

The Lord is faithful in keeping His promises. If He says it, you can believe it, because it's going to happen. If the story of Abraham teaches us anything, it teaches us that we must believe God's Word no matter what.

But like Abraham, for some reason, we think we need to help God out, give Him a hand. Let me give you one example: "I am confident of this, that the one who began a good work among you will bring it to completion by the day of Jesus Christ" (Philippians 1:6, NRSV).

This is a promise from God to us. But what do we do? We fret and worry about what kind of person we are, wonder if somehow we can ever be good enough to make it across the finish line, to make it into the kingdom before that door of probation finally closes on us. Will we ever be able to conquer that one last sin before He comes?

And we take that verse and we twist it to read, "I am confident of this, that even though God began a good work in me, *I will bring it to completion by the day of Jesus Christ*."

It's no wonder that all through the Bible God calls for His people to circumcise their hearts. Like Abraham, we just can't stay out of God's business. For some reason we feel that there is no way that God is powerful enough to keep this kind of promise in a person like us. So we try to help God out, and, like Abram, we just complicate things and make it more difficult for God, for ourselves, and for the people around us.

He promised it; He'll complete it. It's a done deal. Stop worrying and start believing. Every promise in the Bible is ours. We just need to trust that God will be the one to fulfill it. You can't fulfill a promise from God any more than you can fulfill your own salvation. His promises are His business; stay out of it and let Him bless you the way He's promised to bless you.

And finally, there is a promise in the Bible that, as we can tell by looking around us, has yet to be fulfilled. Jesus said that He isn't going to leave us here. He said that He is going to go and prepare a place for us, build us a dwelling place, and that when He is ready, He is going to come and get us, so that we can live with Him forever.

It's been a long time since He made that promise, hasn't it? Generation after generation have sworn that the world has gotten so bad that they are sure they will see Him come back. And generation after generation has passed away.

Where is He? Is this last promise ever going to be fulfilled?

"The Lord is not slow about his promise, as some think of slowness, but is patient with you, not wanting any to perish, but all to come to repentance. But the day of the Lord will come like a thief, and then the heavens will pass away with a loud noise, and the elements will be dissolved with fire, and the earth and everything that is done on it will be disclosed" (2 Peter 3:9, 10, NRSV).

Don't lose faith. Don't give up. God promised that He's going to come back and put an end to all of this, and He's going to take us home. And Revelation 2 says that just like Abram, on that day we will get a new name, a name that speaks of a promise kept.

Lord, thank You for being faithful to me even though I'm not always faithful to You. Forgive me when I'm not faithful and patient. Help me to keep my eyes focused on the promise of Your second coming. Help me to be ready for Your return. Amen.

TEMPTATION

"No temptation has seized you except what is common to man. And God is faithful; he will not let you be tempted beyond what you can bear. But when you are tempted, he will also provide a way out so that you can stand up under it."
1 Corinthians 10:13.

I would like to share with you some universal truths:

1. Temptation knows no prejudice.

Temptation is an equal opportunity employer. There isn't a person on this earth who isn't tempted on a frequent basis. The only people on this earth who avoid being tempted are dead people. So if you are breathing, you are susceptible to temptation. No one is above temptation.

I've seen a couple of bumper stickers recently that have confirmed this universal truth. One of them said, *Lead me not into temptation—I can find it all by myself.* The other one said, *Get thee behind me, Satan, and push!*

Even Jesus was not exempt from temptation. While He was on earth, He was visited by the original tempter himself. The Bible says that the devil visited Jesus during one of His weakest moments and tried hard to lead Him into unhealthy and ungodly activities.

So universal truth number one is that everybody goes through the temptation experience—everybody is tempted.

2. Although temptation visits all people, each person is tempted by different things.

If it's true that temptation is an equal opportunity employer, it's also true that what tempts one person repulses another. And what repulses one person may be the ultimate temptation to another.

Hey, be as alluring as you want to be, there are some things that are just not tempting to me. I don't care how you dress them up or how hungry I am, if you put a big bowl of brussels sprouts in front of me and tell me to stay away from them, I wouldn't be tempted to sneak even one.

Some people can experiment with drugs as teenagers and then just leave them alone. Others try it once and have a lifetime struggle on their hands.

A junkie might have a person pass them on the street and offer them some heroin. It may be a temptation that is more than they can resist. If most of us were standing next to them, the thought of sticking a needle in our arm and plunging heroin into our bloodstream wouldn't tempt us in the least.

Universal truth number one is that we are all tempted. Universal truth number two is that we are all tempted in different ways and by different things. And all of us have our weaknesses. For some it may be pornography; for others it's chocolate. For some it may be the socially acceptable temptation of working hard at the expense of our family to get ahead in this world; for others it may be the socially undesirable temptation of flying off the handle, physically and verbally.

The truth is, we all have our weaknesses and we are all vulnerable to temptation.

3. Everyone on this earth (except one person) has not only been tempted but has also fallen to temptation.

All of us have been presented with the opportunity to do good or to do evil. We have all been in the position to choose what our course of action would be. And, at one time or another, all of us have chosen to do evil instead of good.

All of us have been tempted and fallen to our weakness. And for most of us, our weaknesses, our character flaws, seem more like handcuffs than anything else.

The book of Romans says that "everyone has sinned and fallen short of God's ideal." In other words, everyone has fallen to temptation at one time or another.

In another place, the Bible says that if we say that we don't fall to temptation from time to time, we are a liar, and we make God out to be a liar (see 1 John 1:10).

The Bible teaches us, and our experience confirms, that we have all battled with temptation and lost. It's just a universal fact of life that we have to live with. As long as we are drawing breath, we will battle temptation. And on occasion, as we all know well, we will lose the battle.

The great news is that the Bible guarantees us that if we do fall to temptation God is willing to forgive us for our lapse in judgment and remember our sin no more. So even though we will fall from time to time, God is always willing to forgive our sin and look at us as though it never happened. That's called grace.

So with these three universal truths under our belt, the question has to be asked, "What should I do when I am tempted?"

In the next few chapters I will share some suggestions that have helped me along life's path. But one of the best ways to battle temptation is to avoid putting yourself in a position in which temptation is likely to happen.

My son was about 15 months old when he was starting to learn about the word "no." My wife and I actually had only a couple of things in the house that he was not allowed to touch. Every time he touched them, we took his hands, made him look in our eyes, and firmly said, "No." Sounds authoritative, doesn't it?

One of the things he wasn't supposed to touch was the gas fireplace in our living room. Usually we kept an ottoman wedged in between the couch and a chair in front of the fireplace so that he couldn't get to it.

But guess what my son would do when we'd move it for some reason. He'd walk over and start to look at the fireplace. Then he'd look at us to see if we were looking. When he'd see that we were looking, he'd start to touch the wall all around it, until finally he'd reach in and grab the gas knob and try to give it a crank. He did this with a defiant grin on his face.

When we had barred access to the fireplace, Cole was never tempted to touch it. It didn't even cross his mind. As adults, we are like that also.

One of the secrets to overcoming temptation is not to place yourself in temptation's way.

Martin Luther once said, "Don't sit near the fire if your head is made of butter."

Avoid the places, people, and situations that increase the likelihood of your particular temptation, and you will be more successful in your battle with it.

When Jesus' friends asked Him to teach them how to pray, one of the lines He suggested that they pray was "lead us not into temptation." This line is actually a request for God to lead us in such a way that we avoid tempting situations when possible.

So one of the best ways to battle temptation is to avoid it if possible.

Dear Father, lead me not into temptation, but deliver me from evil. Amen.

FROG IN A POT

"Elijah went before the people and said, 'How long will you waver between two opinions? If the Lord is God, follow him; but if Baal is God, follow him.'" 1 Kings 18:21.

In the previous chapter I shared the first secret to overcoming temptation: Avoid putting yourself in a place where your particular temptation gets stronger. But suppose we do find ourselves in a place or a position to be tempted. In that case it becomes very easy to rationalize away the danger of giving in to the temptation we are dealing with at the time.

Temptation begins to be most effective when we find ourselves in a place where our desire is easily accessed. It's interesting to listen to some of the young people who come into my office and lament a broken relationship. Many of them lament because they let the physical part of their relationship get way out of hand for their level of commitment and maturity.

When I ask them how they got to the place where temptation overcame them, the answers are typically the same: First, they found themselves alone in a warm, dark, cozy place. (Rarely does a young person first cross the lines of a physical relationship when in public or in a group. As we've already discussed, temptation is so much more effective when we find ourselves in a place where what we want is easy to access.) Then, invariably, they will say that they started to rationalize about what they were tempted to do. They said such things as "Well, there's really nothing wrong with this or that." Another thing they said was "As long as we don't go 'all the way,' there's nothing wrong with what we are doing. After all, we do love each other."

Before they know it, they've rationalized their way out of virginity and into an active sex life.

It's so easy to rationalize by saying to ourselves, "Well, it's not like I'm a bad person. After all, I could be doing a lot worse things." Or "I'll do it just one more time, and then I'll quit." My favorite is "If I just do it in moderation, there is nothing wrong with it."

If you find yourself having to rationalize your behavior, then temptation has already won more than half the battle.

It's like the old story about the frog in the pot. (I don't know if this is actually true, and it's kind of gross, but it serves my purpose here.) It's said that if you throw a live frog into a pot of boiling water (do not try this at home), it will hop out and hobble away. But if you put a live frog in a cold pot of water and then slowly heat the water, it will boil to death and never even know it was in danger.

Every time we rationalize our behavior it gets easier to do what we shouldn't the next time. Every time we compromise on what we listen to, what we watch, what we say, or whom we associate with, we become that frog in the pot.

Instead of compromising or rationalizing, look into God's Word, the "perfect law of God" (see Psalm 19:7), and measure what you want to do by that. You will find that each time you stand up for what you believe in, you will be stronger and more up to the task the next time.

God isn't calling a people who are going to waver and rationalize about their choices. Just as Elijah confronted the people of Israel in today's text, God is asking His people, "How long are you going to waver [rationalize] between two opinions? If God is the Lord, then follow Him."

Father in heaven, help me to stand strong for You today. Help me to stop rationalizing my behavior and make right choices that will honor You. Help me to keep trying even when I feel like a failure instead of giving in to the temptation. Through You, I can be strong. Amen.

GET THEE BEHIND ME, EVIL TEMPTER!

"Flee the evil desires of youth, and pursue righteousness, faith, love and peace, along with those who call on the Lord out of a pure heart." 2 Timothy 2:22.

In the two previous chapters you've read two suggestions on how to deal with temptation. The third lesson I'd like to suggest about temptation is to flee from it.

The Bible never tells us to resist temptation. It tells us to flee from it. In other words, don't even get into a conversation with temptation. The moment you start to think about and rationalize what you are being tempted with, the battle is almost over.

I read a story this week about a farmer who saw a country boy lying under one of his apple trees. The farmer yelled out, "Hey, boy, what are you trying to do, steal my apples?"

The little boy kept looking at the ripe apples and yelled back, "No, sir, I'm trying not to."

The Bible tells us again and again to flee from the stuff that wants to get its hooks in us. Flee from immorality, flee from idolatry, flee from youthful lusts.

Walking away from a potentially tempting situation will help you avoid any need to rationalize or fall to what could potentially be harmful to you physically, mentally, or spiritually.

Joseph learned this concept well. If anyone ever had a reason to yield to temptation, it was Joseph when faced with the seduction of Potiphar's wife. After all, every evidence he could sense told him that God had abandoned him. He'd been ridiculed by his brothers, beaten up and thrown into a pit, and sold into slavery in a foreign land.

And she was beautiful. And she was his boss. At first it was just a glance, a little smile, an incidental rub as she passed by. Then it became more obvious. She wanted him, and she didn't keep it a secret anymore. Every day her advances got more obvious, and every day Joseph tried his best to ward off her advances.

Finally one day she cornered him in a room he was cleaning. There was no wriggling out of the situation this time. It was decision time. What was he going to do?

In times of decision-making, one could make a list of the pros and cons of a decision. If Joseph did this, it might play out something like this:

Pros:	Cons:
• She is beautiful, and I'm a young man with natural desires. • It seems as if God has abandoned me. • Nobody will ever know if I do it. • She is my boss, and I'm supposed to respect my master. • Maybe if I do this, I could have an easier life because she will favor me.	• I've been brought up not to yield to this kind of temptation. • I will not be true to myself and what I know is right if I do this thing. • I may not feel as if God is in my life right now, but I know He's there. • This activity would not honor God or His Word.

Most of the young men I know would rationalize their decision away. It would be a no-brainer. But not Joseph. The Bible tells us that Joseph fled from the temptation. In the midst of a horrible set of circumstances, Joseph held on tight to his integrity. He fled temptation because he knew it was the right thing to do.

What about you? What is it that is trying to dig its hooks into you? Are you fleeing from it or entertaining the thought of it? Who are you going to be in the midst of the storm?

Dear God, give me the strength to flee when I need to flee. Keep me away from the situations that put me in danger of losing my integrity. And help me not to rationalize my way into a bad situation. In Jesus' name, amen.

THE EMPTY CHAIR

"Remain in me, and I will remain in you. No branch can bear fruit by itself; it must remain in the vine. Neither can you bear fruit unless you remain in me."
John 15:4.

In the previous three chapters we have been learning how to deal with temptation. In this chapter I'd like to conclude our four-chapter foray into the subject by suggesting that the best weapon against temptation is to practice God's presence in your life. Let me explain.

When I was a teenager, much to the chagrin of my parents, I started dating. I was young and didn't have the moral base I needed to make good decisions about having a girlfriend. In fact, I had never been told that a person my age had no business dating anyone.

One evening, while my parents and sister were away, my girlfriend decided to come over and visit. Now my mom had told me what was appropriate behavior with a girl and what was definitely inappropriate behavior. So I had some principles . . . I did!

Well, the fireplace was going, the curtains were drawn, music was playing, and the girl and I were on the couch together.

All of a sudden I was very, very weak. Temptation was there right in front of me. I rationalized that I probably loved her, and that since she loved me, what could be so wrong?

I was very weak. Temptation was strong, and I was going to lose the battle.

And then I saw the familiar bounce of headlights shine through the front curtains. My mom and dad were driving up. Where *I was once very weak, I was now extremely strong.* Temptation wasn't even an issue with me anymore. I was done rationalizing. Temptation ceased to have a hold on me.

Why? The presence of my parents. It became a stronger influence in my decision-making than the temptation I had so easily fallen to just moments before.

In much the same way, practicing the presence of God in our lives on a daily, moment-by-moment basis can give us the strength to overcome temptation when we would otherwise be weak.

The only way I was going to get back into the same situation with that girl was going to be if my parents left the house again. The only way I can fall to temptation that would have me doing morally wrong things as an adult is if I decide to push the presence of God out of my life.

Walking with God, practicing His presence in our lives, is the key to overcoming all kinds of temptation. It's the key to living a life free of the handcuffs we can so frequently put around our wrists.

Brennan Manning (one of my favorite authors) tells the story of a priest who visits a dying parishioner in his home. (I'm telling the story from memory, so there may be a variation or two from how he tells it.) When the dying man's daughter let the priest enter the room, he saw that there was an empty chair next to the man's bed. The daughter left, and the priest asked, "Were you expecting me?" as he motioned to the empty chair.

"Oh, that," said the man. "Shut the door—I don't want my daughter to hear. All my life I've had a hard time praying. I just never felt as though I connected with God on any kind of personal level. So I asked my priest to help me learn how to pray. He gave me a book from his library by some philosopher/theologian. I had to look up 12 words in the first four paragraphs. I gave the book back and said, 'Thanks [for nothing].' A friend of mine noticed that I was bothered by something, so I told him my dilemma. He told me to take some time every day, put an empty chair across from me, and pretend Jesus was sitting there in the chair. I was supposed to talk to Him as though He was there, as I would a friend. I started to do that, and that's how I've been praying ever since. Just don't tell my daughter—she already thinks I've lost my mind."

The priest gave a blessing to the man and left.

Several days later the priest called the daughter of the dying man to check on him. She shed a little tear and said that he'd passed away that afternoon. And then she added, "But there was something a little odd."

"What was that?" the priest asked.

"When I found my father, his head was lying in that empty chair next to his bed."

Father in heaven, may I find a way to connect with You on a daily basis. I want Your presence in my life each day, but I need Your help. And may Your presence keep me from the sin that so easily entangles me. Amen.

JELLYFISH HURT

*"And in the church God has appointed first of all apostles,
second prophets, third teachers, then workers of miracles,
also those having gifts of healing, those able to help others, those with
gifts of administration, and those speaking in different kinds of tongues."*
1 Corinthians 12:28.

I was walking around a track with my friend Bob Curren a few years back. He is an accountant, and I am a youth pastor. As he was excitedly talking about his job, I got a sour look on my face and interrupted him.

"I can't think of anything worse in the world than to have your job. Sitting in an office and having people mad at you all the time because some number got misplaced on a spreadsheet . . . yuck!"

Bob stopped, looked at me, and started laughing. "I can't think of a worse job than the one you have. Having to deal with hormonally overcharged teens all the time, standing up in front of all those people and preaching, counseling teenagers, double yuck!"

That conversation was a not-so-subtle reminder that God has wired us all differently. Another reminder happened in Mission Bay, San Diego.

I was on a "discover my birth family" trip with my birth mother and some other family members when the suggestion was made that we stop in Mission Bay and rent sailboards. For those of you not fortunate enough to try this horrible sport, a sailboard looks like a surfboard with a sail attached to it. Sailboarders stand on the surfboard, pick up the sail, and let the wind blow them all over the bay. It's that easy, right?

After a one-hour lesson, my two cousins Jed and Cody got up on their boards, grabbed their sails, and glided over the waves of Mission Bay as if they were pros. Of course neither of them are six feet six, slightly overweight, and possessing a questionable sense of balance.

I, on the other hand, am all those things. I got up on my board, grabbed my sail, went five feet, and fell into the water. Not one to give up easily, I got back on my board, grabbed my sail again, went five more feet, and fell into the water again.

Imagine watching this go on for 60 minutes of your life. I think everyone on the beach was in stitches as I inched my way out toward the middle of the bay, not realizing that I was going to have to figure out a way back into the beach against the wind. I'd get up and fall, get up and fall, get up and fall. And the last time I fell, I fell into a jellyfish.

I lay on my board and paddled back to shore. My mom looked at my arm and said, "What are all those welts on your arm from?"

"I don't want to talk about it."

We are not all wired the same. My cousins were obviously wired to sailboard. I was not. God gives all of us different gifts. Different things in this world turn us on in different ways. And He did this on purpose.

God filled His church with different kinds of people who possess different gifts to make His church dynamic and exciting. That's why it hurts me so terribly to see people try to stifle the gifts of people in the church who don't fit into their mold of how church ought to be done. Yes, there are appropriate and inappropriate things for different churches and different audiences, but we need to nurture the spiritual gifts of those around us, even if they happen to be wired way differently than we are. After all, if, as Jesus said, the rocks could cry out in praise of Jesus, can't we find a way for each human being to use their gifts to do the same?

Dear Father, help me realize that not everyone is the way You created me. Help me to see that You created the people in my church with gifts specific to them, gifts that are to be used in praise of You. Amen.

JOY

*"Go, eat your food with gladness, and drink your wine with
a joyful heart, for it is now that God favors what you do."*
Ecclesiastes 9:7.

When you think back on all the pleasant memories you've gathered through the years, which one of them carries the most joy? When I thought about this, I had a couple of great memories to choose from. But the one I had to settle on was my wedding day.

My wedding day was a joy-filled day for lots of reasons. Wendy and I had really been through a whirlwind engagement and had had enough life experiences to make our choice of each other a comfortable one. I know that every wedding day is anticipated, but I couldn't wait for my wedding day. I couldn't wait to be married to the one person I wanted to live with for the rest of my life.

When the day finally came, I did the usual things to be ready for the wedding. I showered, shaved, and got into my rented tuxedo. I drove to the church and met all of the people in our wedding party. People kept coming up to me and asking me how I was feeling. I was honest and said, "I feel excited, lucky, and glad that the day is finally here."

Finally our moment came, and the pastor, my best man, and I walked out onto the platform. The family had been ushered in, the attendants were in their places, the Bible boy and the flower girl had done their thing . . . the only person missing was the bride.

Up until that moment I had been calm, cool, and relatively in control of my emotions. And then the music started, the doors swung open, and there stood Wendy.

Like I said, until that moment, I was calm and confident. When I saw her starting to walk up the aisle toward me, I lost it. I started to cry, and my nose started to run. And I didn't have a hanky. Wendy was doing fine until she saw me, and then she started to cry. And then our pastor saw us crying, and he started to cry. There we were, all crying. My pastor had one hanky. He handed it to me, and we kind of shared it for the next few moments.

Why were we crying? Because of joy. We had abundant joy that day. Joy overflowing manifested itself through tears and smiles. When I think of that day—my best friends, my close family members, and my new bride, all in the same place celebrating love—when I think of that day, I think of joy.

When you look at your life, would you describe it as a life marked by joy? If your family were to describe you, judging by the everyday interactions they have with you, would "joy" be one of the words they'd choose?

Joy throbs throughout Scripture as a profound, compelling quality of life that transcends the events and disasters that sometimes advance against God's people. Joy is a divine dimension of living that is not shackled by circumstances. The Hebrew word means "to leap or spin around with pleasure." In the New Testament the word refers to "gladness, bliss, and celebration."

Godly joy looks beyond our current circumstance and settles on the foundation of what our life has in Christ; the fact that we are ultimately loved without condition and accepted by our Creator and God.

Have you ever known somebody that was joy-impaired? I've known a few of them. I have a friend who pastors a church where the members come each week looking like they sucked on sour grapes for breakfast. Any time the church stands to greet each other on a Sabbath morning they cover their faces to protest the people moving around the sanctuary to greet each other.

I had a church member in Canada that, to my knowledge, decided that since a passage of Scripture describes Jesus as a man of sorrows he would take up that mantle as a part of his Christian experience. I once preached a sermon on joy in that church. Afterward I asked him, "John, are you joyful?"

With a somber look he said, "Yes, I'm joyful."

I said, "Well, then, tell your face, 'cause it hasn't heard the good news!"

William Barclay once said that "a gloomy Christian is a contradiction in terms," and that "nothing in all of religious history had done Christianity more harm than its connection with black clothes and long faces."

What gives you joy? What puts an unending smile on your face? Spend time dwelling on those things. Spend time with people who give you warm, joyous feelings. And most of all, wallow in the knowledge that you are deeply and richly loved by your Creator. He's absolutely crazy about you. And that knowledge ought to give you a permanent grin.

Dear Jesus, even though I don't always feel so great about myself, it comforts me to know that You are crazy about me. Thank You for loving me with an everlasting love. Help me to bask in Your love each day so that joy radiates from me to those I meet. Amen.

FASHION STATEMENT

"I put on righteousness as my clothing; justice was my robe and my turban."
Job 29:14.

Does God care about what you wear? Sound like a silly question? Bear with me as we flesh it out.

What we wear is very important to us. I remember when I found out how seriously schools take the issue of what we wear.

In the ninth grade I was, believe it or not, the class clown. One day in assembly the principal announced that on the Tuesday of the next week we were going to have a fifties day. Well, I got pretty excited about getting a leather jacket and slicking my hair back, until my mom informed me that she wasn't about to spend $200 on a jacket for me. I didn't have anything to wear for fifties day. And then it dawned on me. My mom had a whole bunch of clothes left over from growing up in the fifties. I thought it would be kind of funny to find one of her old sock hop dresses, some old shoes and bobby socks, and go to school dressed in fifties attire like a woman. I had long hair that could be fixed up, so I asked my mom to help me with the idea. My mom was a little crazy back then, so she agreed to help me put together a nice outfit and send me to school. My dad just sat in his chair, reading his newspaper and shaking his head. He did that a lot while I was growing up.

Well, the day finally came. I got up early that morning, and my mom made me into the cutest fifties girl who ever lived (at least I thought so). I had a yellow dress, white shoes that we found at Goodwill, bobby socks, and pigtails. The works. When I arrived at school that morning, I was an immediate hit with my friends. Everything was going along really well until the principal walked around the corner. He took one look at me and said, "Go to my office, call your mom, and have her come pick you up. I will not have you dressed like that in my school while I'm still the principal here." So ended fifties day for me.

That day I discovered that what we wear not only has an impact on ourselves, but definitely has an effect on those around us. If you don't believe me, watch and listen while a scantily dressed woman walks by a construction site during lunch hour. What we wear affects the impressions we leave on those around us.

With the frightening thought of me in a dress firmly planted in your mind, I would like you to notice that the Bible has something to say about what people wear. In fact, God has a huge interest in one particular article of clothing that we may or may not be wearing on a day-to-day basis. In most cases the Bible calls the clothes that people wear "robes."

In the book of Genesis it was a special robe that Jacob made his son—which got Joseph beat up and sold into slavery. Joseph's brothers were jealous because in Bible times a fancy robe signified importance, status, and wealth.

The Bible even says that God wears a robe. In Isaiah 6:1 it says: "In the year that King Uzziah died, I saw the Lord sitting on a throne, high and lofty; *and the hem of his robe filled the temple*" (NRSV). That's a big robe.

Not only does God wear a robe, but the Bible seems to indicate that He also has a huge closet full of robes. And in that closet there is a robe for you and me, if we want one.

In the story of the prodigal son, after the young boy came to his senses and came home—hungry, broke, and in rags—Jesus tells us that the father jumped off the porch, ran to his son, and embraced him. When he was done holding and kissing his son, do you remember the first words out of his mouth? The New Revised Standard Version of the Bible says this: "The father said to his slaves, 'Quickly, *bring out a robe—the best one—and put it on him.*'"

The father saw his son not as a failure in rags but as an heir in a royal robe. And as his son was off doing unmentionable things in a far-off land, the father waited patiently for him at home, hoping beyond all hope that his son would come back and wear the robe that his father had reserved for him long ago.

One day Jesus was walking along the beach talking with His disciples when they heard something. At first it sounded like a wild animal who had been wounded or trapped. But as they looked up the hill, they saw, hurling himself down the hill, what looked like a man. He was naked, cut, and bruised. His hair and beard were matted and snarled with a combination of blood and dirt and who knows what else. His eyes reeled out of control. Running and falling at a breakneck pace, this man, whose soul was consumed with demons, made a beeline for the group of intruders who were walking near the cave that he had made his home. As he ran, voices, deep and guttural, hurled out curses and threats. When the disciples saw this, they knew what to do. They stood behind Jesus, poised to run, just in case.

As the man came closer, those who possessed him realized whom they were now in the presence of, and they sent him into violent seizures. The demons begged Jesus to allow them to occupy the herd of swine that were on a nearby hillside. Jesus granted them their wish, and they drove the swine over the cliff.

As we shift the scene back to Jesus, we see the man, naked, huddled up in the fetal position, shaking with fear and bewilderment. Moved with compassion, Jesus clothes the once-tormented man. As the local townspeople come to see what has happened, they find this man sitting at Jesus' feet, dressed and in his right mind.

There's not one of us who hasn't been the prodigal son or, in some sense, the Satan-filled man lying helplessly at Jesus' feet. The Bible describes a person without Jesus as a person who is poor, blind, and naked. And Jesus wants to heal us. He wants to dress us in His robe. He is offering you His robe right now.

And the reason He's able to offer us this beautiful robe of righteousness is that on one dark day some Roman soldiers stripped Him of His robe and put a scarlet robe on Him and mocked Him. And then they nailed Him to a tree. Jesus gave up His robe so that you and I wouldn't have to remain naked to the power of sin anymore. And now He stands, waiting for us to come to Him by any means possible. He waits for us to come back from the far country. He waits, with a white robe of righteousness that was made in eternity, just for you. One size fits all. Are you interested? Are you ready to come back from wherever you are and allow the Father to accept you back into the family? Are you ready for your robe? What else could you possibly want to wear?

Jesus, thank You for Your perfect robe of righteousness. Help me to accept Your free gift. I don't deserve it, but I'm so grateful that You have given it to me. Help me to wear it every day. Amen.

CUPS

"I will lift up the cup of salvation and call on the name of the Lord."
Psalm 116:13.

The Bible uses the word "cup" as a metaphor for a lot of things. Sometimes it describes cups that we don't want to drink from, as in the two texts below:

"On the wicked he will rain coals of fire and sulfur; a scorching wind shall be the portion of their cup" (Psalm 11:6, NRSV).

"Then another angel, a third, followed them, crying with a loud voice, 'Those who worship the beast and its image, and receive a mark on their foreheads or on their hands, they will also drink the wine of God's wrath, poured unmixed into the cup of his anger, and they will be tormented with fire and sulfur in the presence of the holy angels and in the presence of the Lamb" (Revelation 14:9, 10, NRSV).

I don't know anybody who wants to take a sip out of either of those cups. And then there are the cups that we love to drink from:

"The Lord is my chosen portion and my cup; you hold my lot. The boundary lines have fallen for me in pleasant places; I have a goodly heritage" (Psalm 16:5, 6, NRSV).

"Even though I walk through the darkest valley, I fear no evil; for you are with me; your rod and your staff—they comfort me. You prepare a table before me in the presence of my enemies; you anoint my head with oil; my cup overflows. Surely goodness and mercy shall follow me all the days of my life, and I shall dwell in the house of the Lord my whole life long" (Psalm 23:4-6, NRSV).

That's a pleasant cup—one that all of us love to drink from. So what's in your cup?

I guess the answer to that really depends on what's happening in your life right now, doesn't it? Sometimes we don't really have any control over what gets poured into our cup. We just have to drink what's there. And sometimes our cup can hold a bitter drink. Jesus experienced that.

In Matthew 26 Jesus knew that He was probably experiencing the last hours of His life. He'd been betrayed by a friend and had been plotted against in the most hideous ways. His time was short, and He knew it. When He and His friends finally reached the garden, He looked at them and said, " 'I am deeply grieved, even to death; remain here, and stay awake with me.' And going a little farther, he threw himself on the ground and prayed, 'My Father, if it is possible, *let this cup pass from me*; yet not what I want but what you want' " (Matthew 26:38, 39, NRSV).

Have you ever prayed that prayer? Has the enemy ever poured his bitter drink into your cup, leaving you to drink alone and in anguish? Has your cup ever been filled with the kinds of things that rob you of your sleep—things that dominate your thoughts so thoroughly that you aren't sure if you can take another sip?

When I was 19 years old, my mom developed a brain tumor. I remember those days. I wasn't really a religious person back then, but I remember begging God not to make me and my family drink from that cup. That was a hard cup to drink from.

You know the cup I'm talking about, don't you? I want to remind you of something. We never drink from the cup of bitterness alone. Jesus sat with His disciples and held up His cup of bitterness and said, "Take, drink, this is my blood shed for you." And they drank, from the same cup, together.

When we choose to let Christ be the author and finisher of our faith, we don't drink alone. He drinks with us. He cries with us, He mourns with us, He grieves with us, and He drinks with us because we are His children, and when we hurt, He hurts.

But that's not the only cup we are given to drink. Sometimes our cup is full of good things—the kinds of things that make us want to dance or shout for joy!

I was speaking at a camp meeting in Washington State. I was there alone while my wife was in British Columbia with a young couple in a hospital waiting for our son to be born. I was walking across the camp meeting grounds when a chubby little redheaded cherub rode up to me on his little messenger bike and handed me a little note written on pink paper. The note said, "You're a daddy!" My cup was truly full and has remained full because my son, Cole, is in my life.

You know what it's like to drink from this cup also, don't you? You've been blessed with moments of joy that have given you reason to just break out in a state of uncontrollable grinning.

We love it when our cup is full of blessings from God. We love it when our cup runs over. Aren't those just the best times in life?

The two cups that I just described above, the sour cup of bitterness and the overflowing cup of God's blessings, have something in common. We are not in control of either of them. Most of the time we cannot control the way the winds of strife or the winds of joy blow in and out of our lives.

The fact is that life on this earth is pretty unpredictable, and your cup will be filled from time to time with the bitter and the sweet. That's no mystery. We've all experienced both. And what ultimately counts isn't what *life* pours into your cup but what you choose to put in your cup on a daily basis that will make what life gives you worth living through.

In John 4 we find Jesus sitting at a well having a conversation with a woman who had a cup that, for most of her life, had been overflowing with pain and bitterness. Jesus offered to fill her cup with something more satisfying, something that would replace what was in her cup up to that point.

"Jesus said to her, 'Everyone who drinks of this water will be thirsty again, but those who drink of the water that I will give them will never be thirsty. The water that I will give will become in them a spring of water gushing up to eternal life'" (John 4:13, 14, NRSV).

There is one thing that you can choose to put in your cup. You can drink from it every day. It's called the Water of Life. When we choose to drink from the well of living water, we choose to never drink alone. Whether life hands us a cup full of pain or a cup brimming with joy, we will be sharing our cup with a Brother, a Savior, a Friend.

And when we choose to fill our cups every day with living water, we can look forward to the day when we will share a cup of new wine at a big banquet table with the very source of that living water, our Friend and Savior Jesus Christ.

Jesus, my cup is overflowing with blessings, but at times it overflows with pain. Whatever You put in my cup, help me to realize that as long as I have You in my life, I will never drink alone. Help me to count my blessings and look for Your guidance in my life. Amen.

WHOA, BEAR, WHOA!

"The Lord God said, 'It is not good for the man to be alone.
I will make a helper suitable for him.'"
Genesis 2:18.

One of the joys of working in a small parochial school in the-middle-of-nowhere British Columbia was seeing city kids come to be a part of our program. One of these young people was a kid named John Betita. John grew up in the suburbs of Seattle and hadn't been in as rural a place as Bella Coola.

One Saturday afternoon a group of students and I went on a little jaunt up to the town dump. That might not sound so fun to you, but in Bella Coola the town dump is a source of great entertainment. During the spring and summer months it is loaded with bears eating all the garbage.

On this particular day 14 of us ventured down the dirt road toward the dump to watch the bears climb in and out of discarded automobiles, eat old watermelon rinds, and suck whatever they could find out of old chili cans. As we were walking, something happened that I will never forget for as long as I live.

Two cubs ran out of the bushes just behind us. They were cute and cuddly looking. The problem is, where there is a cub, there is a mama bear. Do you know the reputation of mama bears?

Something that sounded like woofing jerked our heads around away from the cute little cubs and toward the mama bear standing on her hind legs about 50 yards directly in front of us.

I yelled out, "Everybody get real close to each other and don't run!"

Everyone linked arms and just stared as the mama bear got down on all fours and started to charge us at breakneck speed.

John was standing next to me, and he did something that I laugh about to this day. He took his jacket off and wrapped it around his arm, and then he stuck it out as a barrier between himself and the bear.

The bear charged at us until she saw how many of us there were, at which point she dug in and came to a dead stop and ran toward the woods.

After the incident I started to laugh at John. He looked at me with a smile on his face and said, "What?"

"John, if that bear had kept coming, it would have taken that arm you had sticking out, torn it off, and beat you over the head with it."

John, still laughing, asked, "Then what stopped her?"

I replied, "Bears have bad eyesight. When she got close enough to see how many of us were in front of her, she knew she needed to head another direction."

In the Bible the word for "community" is *ekklesia*. Translated into English, the word means "church." God's intention is that we should not be alone. His intention, the way He created us, is for us to be a part of a body of believers, something larger than ourselves. This will not only strengthen our faith but also help protect us from the evil one.

Father, help me to appreciate Your church. Help me to understand that when I worship with other believers You are there. Help me to contribute to Your church and make it stronger because of my participation in the fellowship of believers. Amen.

EMERGENCY, EMERGENCY! COME RIGHT AWAY!

"From him the whole body, joined and held together by every supporting ligament, grows and builds itself up in love, as each part does its work."
Ephesians 4:16.

When Wendy and I worked in British Columbia, we had a dormitory full of adventurous guys who loved to hike, climb, and traverse. Just behind our residence was a saddle between two mountains that made a spectacular waterfall. Two of the boys, Tye and Jimmy, came in and asked if they could go rock-hopping at the base of the waterfall. I told them they could as long as they stayed together and were back by supper. So off they went.

About four hours later Tye came running into the dorm in a panic. "Jimmy's hurt really bad, and he needs help!"

"What happened?" I asked.

"He slipped off a rock [rock is an understatement—they were boulders the size of tanks] and is in the river, and he's stuck. We can't get him out! I think his leg is broken! Come on!"

Wendy got on the phone and called the ambulance, my assistant dean started calling church members, and all the guys and girls in the dormitory started up the steep trail to where Jimmy and Tye had been playing.

When we finally reached Jimmy, we were about a mile and a half up the river. His leg was wedged and stuck between two boulders with ice-cold water rushing over him, bringing his body temperature dangerously low. He was still alert but was in excruciating pain.

A few of us managed to get down to him with some blankets, but we were unable to get him out of his predicament. One group circled up and started praying at the side of the trail. Another group sat on the rocks above and beside Jimmy, giving him words of encouragement and trying to keep him warm.

Finally the EMTs showed up and assessed the situation. They came up with a plan to get Jimmy's leg (still attached to him) out from between the rocks. It was a complicated plan that actually put them and those of us helping Jimmy at a little bit of risk. It was exhausting and took a bit of time, but finally, amid the screaming and wailing of Jimmy's pain, we were able to free him and place him on a stretcher (on top of a rock in the middle of a raging river). Now we had to find a way to get Jimmy and the stretcher off the rock in the middle of the river and onto the trail. Of course, we still had a mile-and-a-half walk down the trail to the road where the ambulance was waiting. Oh, and did I mention that it was now dark?

By now the whole church and community was in on the fun. Everyone was supplied with flashlights and was illuminating the scene like a roadside construction site. We had rigged a way to transfer Jimmy safely to the trail and with considerable effort were able to do so. The EMTs were exhausted. Jimmy was heavy, and every time his stretcher was bumped or tilted wrong he wailed in pain.

The walk down the trail was slow and tedious. One by one people switched to give the stretcher bearers a break. Everyone participated in the rescue of Jimmy Dixon. Finally we got him down to the ambulance and into the emergency room, where Jimmy received lots of pins in his leg along with a fancy cast.

The point is obvious, right? It took a whole community to ensure the safety of one of its members. That's how God designed the church—to work as a community for the betterment of the individual. And that's why it's important to be an active participant in a local community of believers, adding your wonderful gifts to the body of Christ. And that's why it's so tragic when a believer decides he doesn't want to be a part of the family anymore. Finally, the church can protect a believer from Satan, that roaring lion, because there is strength in numbers.

"Let us not give up meeting together, as some are in the habit of doing, but let us encourage one another—and all the more as you see the Day approaching" (Hebrews 10:25).

Father in heaven, please find ways to use me in Your church to strengthen and advance Your kingdom. Amen.

GORILLA FEAR, PERFECT LOVE

"There is no fear in love. But perfect love drives out fear, because fear has to do with punishment. The one who fears is not made perfect in love."
1 John 4:18.

O nce upon a time there was a guy who owned a large gorilla. He kept him in a cage in his basement. He wanted to go on vacation, so he asked his neighbor if he wouldn't mind taking care of the gorilla while he was out of town. His neighbor agreed, so he spent some time showing him how to feed and water the oversized primate. When he was finished, the owner of the gorilla turned and looked straight at his neighbor. "Listen," he said, "whatever you do, don't touch the gorilla."

"Why?" the neighbor asked. "What would happen if I touched the gorilla?"

"Never mind about that—just don't touch the gorilla."

With that the man left for his vacation, leaving his gorilla in the care of his neighbor.

For the first few days everything went quite smoothly. The neighbor fed and watered the gorilla when he was supposed to, and the gorilla seemed reasonably happy.

But one day when the man went down the stairs and approached the gorilla's cage, he noticed that the gorilla was asleep and that his fur was sticking out beyond the bars of the cage. The man thought to himself, *H'mmm, I wonder what gorilla fur feels like.* He remembered the stern warning from the owner of the gorilla, but then he thought, *He's asleep. He'll never know I touched him.* So, ever so lightly, the man brushed the tips of the gorilla's fur with his fingers.

Suddenly the gorilla jumped up in an uncontrollable rage and started yanking on the bars of the cage. To the man's amazement, the gorilla actually bent the bars enough so that he could get out and chase him.

In a panic he raced up the stairs, the gorilla close at his heels. The man ran out the front door at a blistering pace, not able to shake the angry gorilla. In a split second the man glanced over his shoulder to see where the gorilla was and in so doing tripped over a curb on the street and fell into a submissive mass.

The gorilla took a giant leap and landed right over the frightened man. Then the gorilla leaned over, touched the man, and said, "You're it!"

Fear. It's quite an emotion, isn't it? In some instances it can save a person's life. Psychologists call the response that fear brings into a person's life the fight-or-flight response. This is the kind of reaction that causes a person to run from danger or flee to defend their life. So fear can be a valuable emotion.

But fear can also be a debilitating emotion, one that squelches the vitality of life. Last week I decided to surf the Internet in search of statements about fear and phobias. I found an interesting list of just about every phobia ever diagnosed. These are fears that people actually sought professional help to overcome. See if you can recognize what some of these are:

- claustrophobia—fear of confined spaces
- acrophobia—fear of heights
- arachnophobia—fear of spiders

Now here are some that maybe you've never heard of:

- arachibutyrophobia—fear of peanut butter sticking to the roof of the mouth
- alliumphobia—fear of garlic
- cyberphobia—fear of computers
- Dutchphobia—fear of Dutch people
- ecclesiophobia—fear of church
- hippopotomonstrosesquippedaliophobia—fear of long words
- homilophobia—fear of sermons

These are all true phobias that have invaded real people's lives and thrown them into sometimes lifelong therapy.

Although these kinds of fears are real, life-altering phobias are not a threat to the average person. The kinds of fears we deal with on a daily basis are considered more normal, or socially accepted.

Most people get a little nervous on the upper tiers of a tall ladder. It's natural to walk a little faster when you find yourself in a cemetery in the middle of the night. These kinds of fears are all part of a normal existence.

And then there are childhood fears. Do you remember what you were afraid of when you were a child? I didn't learn how to swim until I was 13 because I was afraid of the water. I suppose the fact that I nearly drowned when I was a toddler may have instilled that fear into my life. My fear of water was powerful, but not half as debilitating as my fear of the dark.

When I was a kid, I had a vivid imagination that worked overtime as soon as the lights went out in my bedroom. I don't know if you imagined things in your room when you were little, but I had stuff in my closet and under my bed.

Even more terrifying than that was our carport and backyard. Every couple of days my mom would ask me to take the garbage out. I would have to take the garbage out around the side of our house through the back fence to the garbage cans. I would run as fast as I could, singing "Jesus loves me" as loud as I could, until I got to the can in the backyard. And then I would stand there and try to tell myself that there was nothing in the garbage can that would jump out and get me when I lifted the lid.

I was terrified of the dark.

It's easy to look back and laugh at the fears of our childhood . . . until we realize that the fears of our childhood are replaced with the all-too-real fears of adulthood. Fears of the boogeyman and fear of the dark are replaced by the fear of failure or the fear of an uncertain future or the fear of loneliness. Living in today's world presents us with a whole slew of uncertainties that when dwelt upon can paralyze the most rational person. It becomes so easy for us to allow fear to intimidate our lives.

I can't tell you how many parents I've had in my office, scared stiff about their teenage boy or girl and the decisions they were making. I've had parents living in fear that they wouldn't be able to provide financial support for their families. On the flip side, teenagers are often afraid of telling their parents the truth when they make a mistake. Teenagers are fearful of not getting good grades, not finding a girlfriend/boyfriend, or not having any friends.

If we are honest about it, there are plenty of reasons in our life to be fear-filled people. Because it seems that when it comes right down to it, this life offers us no guarantees. And when you look at the whole concept of fear, the common denominator beneath every phobia and every childhood or adult fear is a basic fear of the unknown.

It's not the dark that a child is afraid of—it's that unknown thing that may be hiding in the dark. Fear of the unknown, fear about what the future holds, is at the root of all our fears. And living in a precarious, unpredictable world doesn't help to alleviate these fears at all.

The Bible says some interesting things about how to deal with fear. "There is no fear in love. But perfect love drives out fear" (1 John 4:18).

I guess the clearest way to illustrate what this means is to look directly at the life of Jesus. If anybody had a reason to be a fearful person, it was Jesus. The expectations surrounding Him and His ministry would have driven the best of us toward some sort of debilitating fear of failure. He was constantly under attack by authority figures and was clearly headed toward an uncertain future.

What was it that gave Jesus the boldness to walk through the darkest hours of this earth's history and not cave in to fear? Perfect love (1 John 4:18).

A songwriter named Michael Card asks, "Why did they nail his feet and hands? His love would have held him there." It was Christ's perfect love for us—His creation—that gave Him the backbone to face the most fearful situation imaginable and walk through it boldly and victoriously. And it's by taking His example that we can boldly face our personal fears and emerge victoriously on the other side of them. It's by developing a tenacious love for God in our lives and an unyielding love for each other that we can find strength similar to Christ's, a love that is stronger than the fear that can so easily dominate our thoughts and decisions.

And make no mistake, the only source of this fear-smashing love is Jesus Christ. It is by allowing Him to reign supreme in our lives that we can develop the strength of fear-conquering love in our hearts. Perfect love cast out fear!

By the way, the only time I wasn't afraid when I had to take the garbage out at night was when my dad walked out there with me. When Dad walked with me, I wasn't afraid. Get the parallel? When we are walking with the Father, we have no reason to fear.

Dear Jesus, please don't let my fears hold me back from doing what You want me to do or being who You want me to be. Amen.

OUT OF GAS

"The man of integrity walks securely,
but he who takes crooked paths will be found out."
Proverbs 10:9.

Someone once said that your integrity is defined by what you do when no one is looking. The children of Israel were being good boys and girls until Moses went up the mountain to meet with God. When they thought they weren't under the watchful eye of Moses anymore, when they thought they were by themselves, out popped the golden calf. Of course, Moses came back down the mountain, and they got busted.

It seems that a lot of us have had to learn integrity the hard way. Like Israel, when we think nobody is watching, integrity goes out the door and we end up doing stuff that, if our parents or people we respected were there, we wouldn't be caught dead doing.

When I was 16 years old, I had a 1968 Pontiac GTO. It was this big muscle car that got about 10 miles to the gallon. Of course, that might have had something to do with the way I drove it. In any case, one Saturday night some friends and I wanted to go cruising in the Seattle area to a place that was occupied by hundreds of teenagers every Friday and Saturday night during the summer.

Our problem was that I had only about an eighth of a tank of gas. Combined, we all came up with about $5, which wouldn't have given us even half a tank of gas. Resa, one of my friends, came up with a suggestion. She said, "I know my mom and dad are in bed. Let's go to my house and siphon some gas out of their tank. Nobody will ever know."

Resa's parents had always been very nice to me. In fact, her dad had been my physician ever since I was a little kid. They had a pretty good hunk of property with horses on it and would let me and my friends ride our motorcycles on their trails, often feeding us and letting us just hang around. When Resa suggested that we siphon gas from one of her parents' cars, I wasn't sure how I felt about it.

In the end, she convinced me that they would be sound asleep and not know a thing. We sneaked onto her property with a gas can and a siphon hose.

I started siphoning and soon had a stream of gasoline gushing from their tank to my gas can. It was about three-quarters full when I heard a noise, turned around, and was blinded by the flashlight. It was Dr. K. He wasn't asleep. He was out on his back deck looking at the stars and heard something unusual coming from the driveway. I was definitely busted. He brought me in and scared me by pondering whether he should call the police or not. Finally, he looked at me and said, "You know, if you would have asked me, I would have given you $20 for gas." I felt pretty low.

I learned a pretty valuable lesson that night. Live your life in such a way that you will never have to worry about getting caught. Live a life with no regrets. Keep your promises. Be honest even when it hurts. Be kind even when you don't feel like it. Show respect even when you are feeling disrespectful.

But most of all, live your life, your public and private life, with the knowledge that you are in the presence of God. Every time you are tempted to act outside of the bounds of integrity, imagine yourself in the presence of Jesus. My mom always told me, "If you can do whatever it is you want to do with Jesus next to you and have Him be proud to be there, then go ahead and do it."

Lord, may I be like You when people are looking and when they aren't. May I be Your follower even when I'm not being observed by another person. May I always be aware of Your presence in my life. Amen.

I WOULDN'T GIVE YOU A PLUG NICKEL FOR THAT!

"As he approached Jerusalem and saw the city, he wept over it."
Luke 19:41.

I once asked a youth group of mine this question: "If there was a fire in your house and every living thing was out of the house safely, and you knew that, what would be the first thing you would grab and haul to safety?"

Years ago I asked my mom the same question. Now, you have to understand my adopted mother before I tell you what her answer was. When I was 19, she had brain surgery that left her both bald and a little crazy.

So I asked her the question. She thought for a second and said, "If I had time to grab only one thing, I think I'd grab my wig and bring that out with me."

Her answer surprised me. I said, "Mom, there are all kinds of things in that house that are worth more than your wig. Why wouldn't you grab the TV or the stereo or some photo albums?"

She didn't take any time to think about her response. "If I'm going to have to stand outside in my bathrobe next to all those good-looking firemen, I'm going to have my hair on. I'm not standing out there to watch my house burn down with no hair on."

Makes sense.

Values are a funny thing. What's valuable to one person may be ridiculous to another. I'm guessing that if you were sitting in my mom's house as it caught fire, the last thing you would grab and carry out with you would be her hair. But for some reason, that's the most valuable thing in my mom's house, to her.

I'm quite sure that many of you wouldn't give me a plug nickel for some of the things that are valuable to me.

I have a jar of udder cream (lotion for cows). I've never milked a cow in my life, but I wouldn't trade my udder cream for a new car. Why? My jar of udder cream was the first gift I ever received from my birth mother. On

132

Christmas Eve we had a gag gift night, and she got me udder cream. Most of you wouldn't want it if I gave it to you, but to me it's priceless.

Here's another item that's worth a bunch to me—a hat that was given to me by the first person I ever baptized. Since then, I've worn it during hundreds of events that I spent with young people. That hat carries with it memories that are more valuable than just about anything in this world—to me.

In the book of Matthew, Jesus says this: "The kingdom of heaven is like *treasure* hidden in a field, which someone found and hid; then in his joy he goes and sells all that he has and buys that field. Again, the kingdom of heaven is like a merchant in search of fine pearls; on finding one pearl of great value, he went and sold all that he had and bought it" (Matthew 13:44, 45, NRSV).

In both of these short parables, people found something they were very excited about, something of great value—to them. When they found what was of great value to them, they went out and *sacrificed everything* in order to have, what was "treasure" to them.

What's valuable to you? What is it that is more important to you than anything on this earth? Do you have a normal value system or a weird one?

I hope that you have a weird one. Jesus did. Jesus had one of the strangest value systems in history. Jesus' value system was so strange that the important "valuable" people couldn't figure it out. They would scratch their heads and say, "How can a man of such good character spend so much time with fishermen, prostitutes, and tax collectors? What kind of values does this man have, anyway?"

I'll tell you what kind of values Jesus had—He had heavenly values. According to my Bible, if there is anything on this earth that is more valuable to us than people, our value system is all messed up and turned around. Jesus valued people more than anything.

Now, some people would challenge that statement and say that Jesus valued the law just as much as or more than He did people. My response to that would be twofold:

1. If Jesus valued the law more than He valued people, He would have cast the first stone at the woman who was caught in adultery (see John 8). He was the only one there that day without sin. He could have cast the first stone. But He didn't.

2. The law says that the wages of sin is death. If Jesus valued the law more than He valued human beings, He wouldn't have laid down His life on the

cross. He would have just let the law do its work of condemning us to death and left us to ourselves.

But Jesus is different than that. To Jesus, you and I are the most important people in this universe.

But it doesn't stop there. Jesus has challenged His followers to adopt the same value system that He has. He told His disciples that the way people would know who they were was by the way they valued and loved each other. It is the same for us today.

What's your value system? What is it that you value more than anything else? And most important, what would the people around you say is your value system? Are you prepared to hear what they would say?

Jesus, give me Your value system. Help me to see things and people in the same light that You do. Help me to never value things over people. Amen.

IS THERE ANYBODY OUT THERE?

"Though he slay me, yet will I trust in him:
but I will maintain mine own ways before him."
Job 13:15, KJV.

He was probably 14 years old when it happened. He should have seen it coming. His brothers hated him from the beginning. As soon as they found out that Daddy loved him best, they hated him. And then there was that coat—a coat that was meant to be a blessing turned out to be a curse. What was Jacob thinking, showing favoritism that blatantly? He made no secret of the fact that Joseph was his favorite. But Joseph grew up dedicated to God. He grew up loving and believing in the God of his father, Jacob; his grandfather Isaac; and his great-grandfather Abraham. He was a 100 percent dyed-in-the-wool believer. At an early age Joseph decided to live for God, and he never really questioned his dedication to Yahweh.

But living for God doesn't necessarily give a person perfect judgment. And in this case, Joseph probably didn't help his cause much. When he had those dreams—the dreams of the 11 stocks of grain bowing to him, and the heavenly bodies bowing to him—he could have kept the dreams to himself. Instead, he chose to tell his brothers, virtually rubbing their noses in the fact that he was Daddy's favorite, and that one day he might get a bigger inheritance than his birth order were to warrant. Remember, he was number 11 in line for inheritance.

It's no wonder that when they got a chance, they threw him into a pit and sold him into slavery. It is a wonder they didn't actually do what they wanted to do—kill him. Now, instead of sitting next to his father and mother in a shaded tent, Joseph found himself in chains, walking behind a camel with gastrointestinal problems. The journey was gruesome. He was hardly fed, and water was only given to keep him alive. By the time he got to Egypt, he could hardly stand on his own two feet.

On the auction block Joseph was sold to the highest bidder, like a used car or a head of cattle. He didn't speak the language, he didn't know anyone in Egypt, and his cries for help fell on deaf ears.

It's easy to be dedicated to God when you are in the safety of Daddy's tent with a pretty colored coat, isn't it? Having good feelings toward God, having a fairly strong faith comes easy when we are experiencing the blessings of God and the comfort of a decent life.

But how easy is it to live for God when your whole world is falling apart? When there is no trace of God, when it doesn't feel like He's there to pick you up and soothe your broken heart. When you pray with all your might and your prayers are met with silence? Or even worse, when your prayer is for deliverance from a problem, and instead of getting what you want, your worst fears are realized? Then what? What happens to your dedication then?

A bad situation got worse. A fellow named Potiphar bought Joseph. One day Joseph was working in the house when he heard something like this: "Hey, big boy. You must be tired, because you've been running through my mind all day."

Joseph looked up, and there she was. It was Potiphar's wife. Easy on the eyes and hardly dressed, she was anything but uninviting. In fact, she was downright gorgeous. Now, you can't tell me that a 17-year-old boy isn't going to be tempted to partake in the fruits of passion when the fruit is that easy to pick.

Joseph looked at her, and the hormones started to race, his brain got a little dizzy, and for a moment the tempter must have said something like "Joseph, it's OK if you indulge this one time. It's not like you would be doing something wrong. After all, she is your boss. You are just doing as she says. It's not like you have a choice."

And the Bible says that this didn't happen just one time. Genesis 39 says that Potiphar's wife was hitting on Joseph on a daily basis, trying every line in the book to get him into bed with her. This was not a one-time temptation. The devil tempted Joseph through this beautiful woman day after day. It's easy to say no once. But having free access to free pleasure in a place where nobody from your church or family will ever be . . . where nobody would ever find out what you've done . . . now, that's temptation.

Joseph could have justified this tempting offer in a million ways so that nobody would have blamed him for what happened. Instead, he stuck to the convictions that he knew God would have him honor.

Finally, the Bible says that she grabbed him, and he fled from her and the house (see Genesis 39:12). He saw that the claws of temptation were about to dig into him, and he fled.

And what was his reward? He was sent to an Egyptian prison. Now, lest you think this was some sort of Egyptian resort, Joseph was thrown into a dungeon with a bunch of other prisoners who had no shower or bathroom facilities. His reward for honoring God was to be thrown into a place filled with the scum of humanity and every smelly thing that came out of them.

Let me reiterate: it's easy to be a dedicated follower of God when you're living in your daddy's tent and wearing a pretty coat. But how easy is it when you keep honoring God with your choices and every evidence you can see suggests that not only does God not care—He may not even exist at all. Where is He? Isn't He supposed to be there for you in your time of trouble? Joseph was rewarded with silence and a worse life than when he had started praying in the first place.

Joseph may have pondered these thoughts, but he never wavered in his faith. He strove to honor God in everything he did, in every choice he made. And like Job, he must have prayed the prayer "Though he slay me, yet will I trust in him."

And in the end? God honored the choices Joseph made. It took some years, but God honored him. He honored the faith that Joseph stuck to, even in the times of God's seeming silence. Most people think that the way God honored Joseph was by putting him in charge of Egypt. If that's what you think, then you've missed the whole point of the story. *God didn't honor Joseph by putting him in charge; God honored Joseph by using him to preserve His people, to lead them out of a destructive famine.*

Listen to Joseph's own words in Genesis 45:5-7: "And now, do not be distressed and do not be angry with yourselves for selling me here, because it was to save lives that God sent me ahead of you. For two years now there has been famine in the land, and for the next five years there will not be plowing and reaping. But God sent me ahead of you to preserve for you a remnant on earth and to save your lives by a great deliverance."

That's what Joseph's reward was. To be used by God to accomplish His purpose. And that will be your reward if you stick with God, even through the hard times.

Father, help me to trust You, even in the hard times. Help me to realize that even in the hard times I am being used by You to fulfill the purpose You've given me in life. Amen.

PURE IN HEART

"Blessed are the pure in heart, for they will see God."
Matthew 5:8.

Somebody once asked me, "If you were to make the decision to completely sell out to God, to fully follow His will in your life, what kind of changes would you make?"

Interesting question. Jesus tackled that question in a talk He delivered on the side of a mountain, which was appropriately called the Sermon on the Mount. It was during this talk that Jesus taught people who were spiritual seekers just what kind of people God wants to make us into.

The first nine statements Jesus made during this talk are all positive ones. Theologians call them the Beatitudes. I'd like you to think about one of the Beatitudes in this chapter. It says, "Blessed are the pure in heart, for they will see God."

The word "blessed" and the word "happy" are the same word in the language the Bible is written in. So, read a different way, it says that people who have pure hearts are happy people, and more than that, they will see God.

What does it mean to be pure in heart? I asked myself that as I was preparing to write this chapter, and I found out more than I wanted to. I looked up the word "pure" in the Greek language to see if I could more closely come up with what Jesus was really trying to say here.

What I found was being "pure in heart" has a few different levels to it.

First and foremost, on a very surface level, a person who is pure in heart is a person who practices telling the truth. To put it another way, a person who is pure in heart isn't a liar.

Do you remember the first time you ever told a lie?

When I was 3 years old, my family lived in Pasadena, California. One day I was out in the front yard playing while my dad worked on the car. As I was playing, I thought I heard the familiar sound of the ice-cream truck coming down the street. I got so excited, I decided to hunt it down and get some ice cream. It wasn't long before I was lost, finding myself in a little café. There was a policeman sitting at the counter. I asked him if he had seen the ice-cream truck. He flipped a nickel on the counter, and the man behind the counter gave me an ice-cream cone. I left and somehow found my way home.

As I came up the driveway, my dad slid out from under the car and asked, "Where did you get that ice cream?" Even at 3 years old, I knew that I'd get a spanking if I told my dad what had happened. So I lied and said that the neighbor had given it to me.

I immediately ran into the house, dropped my ice cream, and started crying. I flew into my mother's arms and told her about the lie I had told.

It seems that from the beginning we somehow start out with hearts that need to go through some sort of purification process. We aren't born with pure hearts. Our tendency from a pretty young age is to lie to get out of difficult situations.

The first character trait that God offers people who strive after a pure heart is basic verbal honesty, no matter the consequence. And the Bible elaborates on this all over the place.

In fact, just a few verses down from this one, Jesus says that when you are asked to make a commitment, let your "yes" mean "yes" and your "no" mean "no." Just leave it at that. Don't go swearing on a stack of Bibles or crossing your heart and hoping to die.

If you have a pure heart, eventually people will view you as a person of your word. And because you are pure in heart, people will know that what you say is never intentionally misleading. You will be a person who tells the truth.

But being pure in heart goes beyond just telling the truth. When the Bible talks about a person's heart, it's not talking about the organ that's beating in a chest. It's talking about the inner recesses of ourselves, the place where we feel deeply, where secret decisions are made. In the Bible our heart is the place where we mix our rationale and our emotional life. Our heart is where we are who we are when all of the pretenses and masks are stripped away. In essence, our heart is our soul, uncovered.

Consequently, being pure in heart means that the deepest recesses of our lives are filled with a godly integrity. People that are pure in heart are people of integrity.

In fact, being pure in heart is synonymous with being a person of integrity. My word processor uses these synonyms for the word "integrity": "credibility," "fidelity," "honor," "nobility," "principle," "character," "decency," "dignity," "guiltlessness."

People who live lives of integrity (pure in heart) are people who live their lives honestly—not only in word, but also in action. Pure-in-heart people have pure motives. They do what they do for the right reasons. There is no hidden agenda, no hook underneath the bait. Pure-in-heart people live their lives, even their secret lives, with integrity and out of a pure motive.

When I was about 11 years old, my mom wanted me to learn what it was like to do nice things just for the satisfaction of doing them. In my neighborhood lived a woman who was 87 years old. She had a hard time getting around and wasn't able to mow her grass very well anymore. So my mom asked me if I wanted to do it.

I said, "Sure. How much will I get paid?"

"Nothing. I want you to do it just to be nice."

I'd never heard of anything so ludicrous in my life. "Thanks, Mom, but I'll pass on the freebee."

"OK," my mom said, "how about if you go mow her lawn for free and I increase your allowance by $10 per week?"

"Deal."

So I went down to Anna's house and mowed her lawn once a week. The whole time she would follow me around and show me the places I missed. She would also make me stop the lawn mower, take a shovel, and rid her lawn of the land mines the neighbor's dogs would leave on a regular basis.

One day after I was finished mowing her lawn, Anna came out to send me off and said, "You are such a nice boy. I don't think I've ever met a young man who would sacrifice an afternoon just to mow an old woman's lawn and not get paid for it."

And without thinking, I responded, "I wouldn't do this for free. If my mom wasn't paying me, I wouldn't even think of doing this."

Her face dropped as she turned and walked back into the house. Her disappointment came from a sense that what I was doing didn't have pure motives. In fact, my motives were tainted to the point that if my mother would have stopped increasing my allowance I wouldn't have ventured near Anna's yard.

One of the things that just seems to come along with being a human being is that we all suffer from tainted motives, at least from time to time. Sometimes this can be benign, but sometimes it can be disastrous.

How many times have we all seen people get married with motives that maybe weren't so pure? How many guys have asked girls out on dates with some sort of hidden agenda or motive? How many business transactions are entered into with little to no integrity on the part of one or both of the participants?

God offers people who want to be pure in heart a life of integrity. He offers us a heart of pure motives—a life in which we choose the right things for the right reasons.

God wants to do that. He wants to give you a pure heart. A life of integrity. Is this something you want from God?

Dear God, give me a pure heart today. Help me to live my life with integrity, even if nobody but You is looking. Amen.

THE WORK OF A LIFETIME

*"Therefore he is able to save completely those who come to God through him,
because he always lives to intercede for them."*
Hebrews 7:25.

One of my least-favorite parts of being a principal is having to be a disciplinarian. I hate it because most of the time my disciplinary committees have to dwell on and deal with the negative behaviors of students and not on the positive.

That being said, there are some parts of discipline councils that I think are very interesting. One of the interesting parts of discipline council is the answers we receive from students when they are asked one specific question.

Here's how it goes. "Why did you do what you did?"

Answer. "I dunno."

Is it truly possible to do something completely wrong and have no idea why you did it? It must be, because as a teenager, that was my most common answer when my mom or dad asked me why I did something. "I dunno."

This answer, "I dunno," is also the answer I get from a lot of Christians whenever I ask them this question: *What's your ultimate goal in being a Christian?*

Most common answer: "I dunno." Second most common answer: "To make it to heaven."

I want to share a couple of texts with you. I hope these texts will do for you what they've done for me—to give you a goal in your spiritual life.

"As obedient children, do not conform to the evil desires you had when you lived in ignorance. But just as he who called you is holy, so be holy in all you do; for it is written: 'Be holy, because I am holy'" (1 Peter 1:14-16).

"Finally, brothers, whatever is true, whatever is noble, whatever is right, whatever is pure, whatever is lovely, whatever is admirable—if anything is excellent or praiseworthy—think about such things" (Philippians 4:8).

"We demolish arguments and every pretension that sets itself up against the knowledge of God, and *we take captive every thought to make it obedient to Christ*" (2 Corinthians 10:5).

I have a Korean friend in the Northwest who didn't know very much English but had a great sense of humor. Whenever I'd present a tough spiritual challenge from the pulpit, he'd say out loud, "Easy to say, hard to do."

Can you imagine what it would be like to take captive *every thought* and make it obedient to Christ?

What would it be like to have the kind of faith that would keep every thought pure, unselfish, and full of love? Can you imagine that? Neither can I.

But that's the challenge the Bible gives us as believers. That's the goal. To be totally sold out in every way possible to Christ.

So from now on, if anyone asks you, "What's your personal goal for being a Christian?" or "Why are you a Christian?" you can say, "My goal is to be totally sold out, totally devoted, in action and in thought, to Jesus."

Easy to say, hard to do.

People who have studied this stuff for a long time have said that "sanctification is the work of a lifetime." In other words, this stuff doesn't happen overnight. In fact, sometimes it seems like it isn't even happening at all—this process called sanctification.

There is a psychologist named Abraham Maslow who talks a little bit about this and has a progressive list of how people grow behaviorally that I think applies here. He says that there are four steps to healthy/good behavior. I think these steps can also apply to our spiritual development. Let's look at them together and see where you fit in.

1. Unconscious Incompetence. Basically, this means that you are so out of it that when you are being an idiot you don't even know that you are being an idiot. In other words, you aren't even aware that what you may be doing is wrong.

In fact, if you are in this stage of spiritual development, it's likely that you don't even know what I'm talking about right now. You are completely oblivious to your sin.

We see this in children. Children do things all the time that they don't even know is wrong. We don't hold this against them; they're children. They haven't learned all the differences between right and wrong.

Unfortunately, a lot of the time grown-ups act the same as children. They are so uninformed about who God is and what He has to offer them that they are oblivious to the fact that their lives are being lived in opposition to God and His will.

2. Conscious Incompetence. This is the stage at which you know when you are doing wrong. You still do wrong, but now you know that what you are doing is wrong. Do you remember the first time you realized that you did wrong?

In a previous chapter I told you about my first lie. It's something that has stuck in my mind since I was 3 years old.

Knowing the difference between right and wrong, moral and immoral behavior, happens to most of us at a pretty early age.

Unfortunately, again, too many people get stuck on this level of spiritual behavior. They go along in life not really paying attention to what they do, watch, or listen to, and after some reflection, they realize they have been doing wrong things—sinning.

When they realize this, they confess and ask for forgiveness, only to have to go through the whole process time and time again.

Most people in this phase of spiritual growth really rely on 1 John 1:9 because they are having to constantly go back to Jesus for the same thing over and over. This phase of spiritual growth can be a frustrating one.

But thank God, our spiritual walk doesn't have to stop there. We can actually grow from there to another step called . . .

3. Conscious Competence. Conscious competence is a good place to be. It means that you know the right thing to do, and most of the time you do what you know is right.

You may not want to do what is right. You may say that you are going to do opposite of what you know you should do. But you end up doing right nonetheless.

It's like the parable of the two sons. The Father asks them both to do something for him. One says, "Sure, Dad, I'll do that," and then walks away and ignores his dad's request.

The next says, "No, I don't want to do what you say," but then goes and does what his dad asks. He knew what was right, and even though he may not have wanted to do it, he ended up doing what was right.

Do you ever feel like that? The people around you really want you to join in on something that you know is wrong. Every fiber in your being is tempted to fall into their pattern of behavior, and you want to do the wrong thing. But in the end, you know the difference between right and wrong. You choose the right, you shun the wrong . . . maybe sometimes even wondering if it's worth the fight.

Well, I'm here to tell you that it is worth it. Choosing right over wrong, good over evil, love over hate, righteousness over sin pays off every time.

When you get in the habit of making right choices, it builds your character. Each time you make a right choice, it makes it easier to do the right thing the next time temptation knocks on your door.

It's like exercising. Each time you go through the pain of working out a muscle, it rebuilds that muscle and makes it stronger the next time you work out.

A lot of mature Christians are at this stage. Maybe you are one of these people. Much of the time you make right choices. Keep struggling. Keep doing the right thing. Don't give up.

And remember, this stage of spiritual development isn't even your goal. Your goal is even higher than this.

4. Unconscious Competence.

Unconscious Competence is when you do right, not because you know it's the right thing to do, but because it has become your nature to do so.

That's where Jesus ended up in His life. He didn't make right choices after a conscious decision to avoid evil, He did right because He was right. It became His nature to do good because He was good.

Maybe you have flirted with this stage of spirituality before. This is how you can tell. Someone comes up to you out of the blue and thanks you for doing something or praises your efforts in some area and your response is a kind of confused "I didn't even realize anyone was watching" response.

The kudos you receive may even seem unjustified. You were just acting normal. Issues of right versus wrong didn't even enter your mind. You just did what you did because you wanted to.

That's kind of what this final goal of spirituality looks like. Doing good because it has become your nature to do good. Acting like Jesus in every situation because it has become your nature to act like Him. Not having to think about it because you have become it.

Now, the question is, where are you in your spiritual growth—unconscious incompetence, conscious incompetence, conscious competence, or unconscious competence?

Wherever you are on the spectrum of Christian growth, just remember, you are God's chosen, the apple of His eye, and He loves you. And He will finish in you that which He has purposed in your life.

Father, live in me so thoroughly that I act like Jesus
even when I'm not trying to. Amen.

BURIED ALIVE!

" 'Don't be alarmed,' he said. 'You are looking for Jesus the Nazarene,
who was crucified. He has risen! He is not here.
See the place where they laid him.' "
Mark 16:6.

One of the wonderful memories I have from working and living in British Columbia is of a campout the little school I served took one February. I'm not sure exactly where we were, but I know we parked and backpacked our things through the deep snow for about a quarter mile off the road to a cabin in the deep woods.

When we got there, the girls set their stuff up downstairs, and the boys took the loft. We were eating supper when Dan, one of my students, said, "Hey, we should sleep outside tonight! Let's dig a big hole in the snow, put our tent in it, and sleep. Besides, all these other people aren't going to let us get to sleep tonight anyway."

I agreed, and we went outside and started digging a huge hole in the snow. It took us a while, but with a lot of determination we finally dug a hole big and deep enough for our two-person dome tent.

When it was time to retire, we said our good nights and disappeared to our quiet little retreat. We nestled into our sleeping bags and started to drift off to a peaceful sleep . . . until the wind started to blow. And it wasn't a gentle breeze that night—the wind was howling and bringing the temperature down to about 35 below. We were freezing. I asked Dan if he wanted to go back into the cabin. He said, "No way—I'm sticking with my decision. I'm staying out here. It'll warm up."

And it did. At least enough for both of us to fall asleep. What we didn't realize was the reason it warmed up was that the wind had blown a bunch of snow into our hole and on top of our tent. We didn't know because we were peacefully asleep in our now-warm sleeping bags.

In the morning Dan and I woke up to the sound of faint voices calling our names. At first we were disoriented. We were warm, but we couldn't move very much because we were pinned in by the snow. Then we realized the voices we were hearing were calling our names—and they were coming from directly above us.

Then the realization hit: we were buried alive. We started yelling and then listening. Finally I heard my wife say, "Shhhh! Did you guys hear something?"

We yelled again. Finally the group, who were standing right on top of us, figured out that we were buried beneath them. They retrieved the shovels we had used to dig our way in and dug us out. Dan and I hopped out of our tent in our mummy bags like Lazarus out of the tomb. I don't think we ever realized how close we had come to suffocating in that tent.

In 1 Corinthians we read that the last enemy to be conquered by Jesus is death. I can't wait for that day. Jesus gave us a little preview of what that day is going to be like when He raised Lazarus from the dead. What an incredible joy it was for Lazarus' family as he came out of the tomb, once dead and then alive.

But nothing can compare to the joy the universe expressed when they saw Jesus rise triumphantly from the grave. Look at what Psalm 24 says prophetically of that wonderful event:

"Lift up your heads, O you gates; be lifted up, you ancient doors, that the King of glory may come in. Who is this King of glory? The Lord strong and mighty, the Lord mighty in battle. Lift up your heads, O you gates; lift them up, you ancient doors, that the King of glory may come in. Who is he, this King of glory? The Lord Almighty—he is the King of glory" (Psalm 24:7-10).

There is only one more event in history that could compete with Jesus' resurrection from the dead. And that's the one told about in 1 Thessalonians 4: "According to the Lord's own word, we tell you that we who are still alive, who are left till the coming of the Lord, will certainly not precede those who have fallen asleep. For the Lord himself will come down from heaven, with a loud command, with the voice of the archangel and with the trumpet call of God, and the dead in Christ will rise first. After that, we who are still alive and are left will be caught up together with them in the clouds to meet the Lord in the air. And so we will be with the Lord forever. Therefore encourage each other with these words" (verses 15-18).

What an exciting day for the universe; what an exciting day for God! That will be the day that His redeemed, the people whom His Son died and rose for, get to spend eternity with Him. And He will be their God, and they will be His people.

Thank You, Jesus, that I serve a living *Savior. Jesus,*
I can't wait to see the promise of Your resurrection fulfilled
in my loved ones who have fallen asleep in You. Amen.

WORSHIP

"Therefore, I urge you, brothers, in view of God's mercy, to offer your bodies as living sacrifices, holy and pleasing to God—this is your spiritual act of worship."
Romans 12:1.

Worship is an interesting animal. Good worship to one person is sacrilege to another. Soon after I gave my heart to the Lord I was invited to go with a friend to a downtown prayer meeting at a place called Chapel of Peace. We went in, were greeted warmly by some church members, and found our way to some seats near the back of the sanctuary.

Everything seemed pretty normal until the music started. When it did, a man jumped up, grabbed the microphone, and started shrieking unintelligible sounds into it. When he did that, the whole place erupted. People were flying everywhere. Scads of them were writhing on the floor, while others did pirouettes down the middle of the aisle. All of them were speaking in loud nonsensical tones.

Suddenly 16 hands were on me and my friend, and the people began to frantically pray over us in their secret language. My friend and I slipped from their grasp and stepped out of the church. It turns out that the Chapel of Peace wasn't very peaceful. Was that worship?

Another experience I've had happened as a student of mine and I were driving from California to British Columbia. We had some vehicle trouble that caused us to have to travel over the weekend, so we decided to stop at a church in northern California and get some good spiritual food.

We stepped into the church and sat down toward the back. Nobody greeted us as we came in. One older gentleman nodded our way as we entered the sanctuary. We sat toward the back because we weren't really dressed for the occasion. Both of us were in the same clothes we'd had on for 48 hours, and we were unshaven and a little greasy.

The church service was ill-prepared, to say the least. The organ sounded like the organist was wearing mittens. Then, after a prayer, someone said, "Gladys is supposed to do a special song for us today. Has anyone seen Gladys? Gladys, are you here?" Gladys never did show up. After that the speaker began to talk . . . and talk. The sermon was interrupted only by the noise of feedback from the 30-year-old sound system. Each time the microphone squealed it woke half the congregation back up. The fellow who was speaking must not have thought his audience was very bright, because he would make a point, illustrate the point, and then explain his illustration, for a really long time. It was agonizing to sit and hear him struggle.

When church was finally over, my young friend and I stood in the lobby and waited to make a new friend or be invited to eat at the potluck dinner that was happening downstairs. Nobody said a word to us.

We left, and got some food elsewhere. Was what happened in that church "worship"?

The fundamental act of worship is an expression of our feelings to and about God. Worship is a verb. It's something we do. Worship varies from culture to culture and from person to person. Worship is really all we have to let God know how we feel about Him. When we don't worship, in essence we are ignoring God. Who is worshipped is important to the devil (Luke 4:7, 8). Whom we worship is important to God (Exodus 20). And worship is very important to Jesus (John 4:23; Matthew 21:12, 13). And one thing is for sure: worship is at the center of what is going to be happening toward the end of earth's history. (In Revelation 13 and 14 the end-time battle for the allegiance of God's people centers on whom we will worship.)

So if worship is so important in the Bible, to God, and to Jesus, and ultimately, if the devil is going to attack God's people over the issue of whom we worship, one question has to be asked: How important is worship to me?

There is really only one way to answer that question. And that's with another question: How often do I worship God? I'm not asking how often you attend church. I'm asking how often you worship God? Once a week? Once a day?

Before you answer definitively, I'd like to suggest some things about worship that you may not have pondered before. First of all, worship is both intentional (practiced) and unintentional (lived).

Think for a moment about unintentional worship. The philosophy behind this idea comes from today's text. Romans 12:1 says that offering our bodies as living sacrifices is an act of worship. In other words, choosing to live a God-fearing life is a constant act of worship. Living a life of integrity, honesty, and kindness is a continual praise offering to God. He sees these things as a sacrificial act of worship. And choosing to walk in the paths of righteousness in our lives is pleasing to God.

Every time we make a decision to do good instead of evil, that's an act of worship. Every time we extend the hand of kindness instead of taking the easy road of ignoring a need, that's an act of worship. All of these things are a part of offering our bodies up as living sacrifices.

God loves this kind of worship. He loves it when His kids choose to extend mercy, grace, and forgiveness. He loves to see His kids choose self-control. And just like an unseen parent who observes their children making good choices and representing the family well, God loves it when we choose the path of Jesus over the path of the world. Just choosing to live a good life is an act of worship.

So I ask the question: How often do you worship God? Maybe it's more often than you think!

During one sermon series on sacrifice, I built a stone altar at the front of the church. That particular weekend we decided to do things a little different. The message was preached first, and then we ended by worshipping God through singing songs of praise and thankfulness to Him. During the praise and worship, I told the congregation that anyone who was thankful for what God had done for them in their lives could bring an offering and lay it on the altar as we sang.

The response was almost overwhelming. People who had never before considered tithe and offering as an act of worship walked up two and three times to lay their "thanks" on the altar. True sacrifice happened that day. So did true worship.

Have you ever thought that your giving is an act of worship? Not only is the giving of money to the cause of God an overt act of worship, so is the giving of your time and energy to God's cause.

So, from now on, consider how you live your life as an act of worship. Are you honoring God with your life, with your choices? Then you are worshipping God. Yes, Bible study, prayer, singing to God, those are also all acts of worship. Intentional acts of worship please God and build faith. But remember, just because you aren't at church or in the quiet little corner of your house doing a devotional doesn't mean your worship has ceased. Your worship continues through the day by how you choose to live your life.

Father in heaven, may my life be a perpetual act of worship. May I worship You on a daily basis instead of once or twice a week. Amen.

MAY MY WILL BE DONE!

"He went away a second time and prayed, 'My Father, if it is not possible for this cup to be taken away unless I drink it, may your will be done.'"
Matthew 26:42.

God's will is a funny thing. Not "ha, ha" funny, but funny in that it's hard to understand. It seems as though the world has an interesting sense of God's will. When a person wins the lottery, the newspaper says that they "got lucky." When hurricane Ike hit Texas, I heard several news reports that referred to it as an "act of God." Is it really God's will that a hurricane damage property and disrupt the lives of millions of people? Probably.

As a pastor I have attended more than enough anointing services. An anointing service is several people gathering around a sick person, praying for them, and anointing them with oil, asking for God to heal them. In each case, somebody in the group will pray fervently for the healing of the sick person and end with the caveat "If it be Thy will." Is it really the will of God that somebody die of pancreatic cancer? Probably.

I had an interesting thing happen in my office just the other day. The whole situation actually started a year or so prior. We had an opening in our school for a new chaplain. In the process, we were trying to figure everything out from finances to personnel alignments. During this time a very capable young woman was available for the job. We interviewed her and found that she could be a great fit. Unfortunately, the way circumstances fell into place, we weren't able to hire her full-time at the school. So the church, wanting her badly to be their youth pastor, asked if the school would pay for half her salary and they would pay for the other half, thus giving her full-time work. As a personnel committee we prayed about the situation, asking for God's will to be done. At the end of the day we decided not to hire her as a half-time chaplain, preferring to wait it out so that we could hire a full-time chaplain down the road.

In the end, the church got a very capable full-time youth pastor and the school hired a wonderful full-time chaplain. It seemed that in the end, God's will had been done . . . until I noticed a poster in my office advertising that the woman we didn't hire was speaking at a youth conference our school was attending later that year. I thought that was a neat coincidence, so I yelled out from my office to a group of people near our front desk, "Hey! So and so is one of the presenters for the youth conference next month!"

One of the people in the lobby who really wanted the young woman hired while we were interviewing her stepped into my office and said (with more than a little aggression), "I'm sure she'll be a success wherever she ends up. We could have had her here! AND *YOU PEOPLE* ARE THE REASON WE DIDN'T GET HER!"

So much for God's will.

I think too often in life we give God credit when things go our way and blame people for messing things up and thwarting God's will when they don't. I think that's a pretty arrogant outlook on life.

I'd like to propose something here that I don't think many Christians will agree with me on: *God sees* everything *that happens in this world and then weaves what happens into the big picture of His ultimate plan.* I would include in this statement hurricanes, tragic deaths, unforeseen accidents, wonderful surprises, unexpected joy, hirings and firings. Everything.

When we ask for God's will to be done and then get sour for what we get, isn't that the same as blaming God for not loving us enough or caring enough about us to get what we want?

I think it would be more prudent of us as Christians to embrace what is set in front of us and play the cards we have been dealt, realizing, believing, and understanding that ultimate resolution is going to happen when He comes back and sets everything right as it should be. Any other attitude assumes that God isn't doing His job and should have arranged things differently. (Aren't you glad we aren't God? We'd just mess everything up!)

Jesus struggled in the garden, "Please take this cup away from Me." But He continued, "Not my will, but Yours be done." It seems that the last thing Jesus wanted was the cross. But He submitted to the will of His Father, as painful as it was. He embraced the cross, and by so doing, He embraced the human race into a saving relationship with Him.

Lord in heaven, help us to do Your will in our lives, even when it's hard.
Help us to remember that all things work together for good,
for those who love and serve You. Amen.

FUN FACTOR

*"Sarah said, 'God has brought me laughter,
and everyone who hears about this will laugh with me.'"*
Genesis 21:6.

Of my many strange personality quirks, my sense of humor is the one that gives me the most enjoyment and gets me into the most trouble.

When I was in seminary, my wife and I lived in a house that had an extra room in the basement. We decided to turn that room into a computer/television room. So we set up the room with a couple of lounge chairs facing the TV (away from the door) and the computer on the other side of the room by the door.

In the course of our busy lives, somehow we misplaced our remote control. So every time we wanted to change the channel or adjust the volume on our television set, we had to get up and do it manually. (I can't believe that Americans had to go through this excruciating exercise all those years before somebody invented the remote!)

Unfortunately, I have just enough ADHD that I can't sit and watch one program without flipping through channels to see what else I'm missing. So one afternoon on my way back from school, I decided to stop and buy another remote.

When I got home, I came through the front door, put my coat on the coat tree, and bopped down the stairs toward the TV room. When I got there, I saw a prime opportunity to have a little fun.

My wife, whose eyes don't work the way they should, was sitting close to the TV and watching an afternoon program. She had found the remote earlier that day and was able to sit in a lounge chair and flip channels. I quickly unwrapped the new remote, put batteries in it, and started my evil little prank.

Standing on the other side of the barely open door, I pointed the new remote at the TV and changed the channel. Wendy cocked her head, looked at the TV, pointed her remote at it, and changed it back. I changed it again. She changed it back.

I hit the channel-up button on my remote and held it there. Wendy looked at her remote, shook it really hard, pointed it at the TV, and turned it off. I turned it back on and turned the volume up to an earsplitting level.

Wendy threw her remote up in the air, started screaming (because she was by then convinced our TV was possessed), and ran out of the room right into me with a new remote and a huge grin on my face.

It took a couple of weeks for the bruises on my chest to go away, but man, did I get a laugh out of that one!

I don't mean to attribute human form to God too much here, but when I read the Bible, I see all kinds of evidence that God loves to laugh. Can you imagine the grin on His face when He thought up and created kangaroos? How about the little smile on Jesus' face when He said, "Hey, Peter, get out of the boat and walk on the water toward Me!" Or how about the time Jesus asked Peter to go catch a fish, open its mouth, and take the coin he found to pay the Temple tax? He must have laughed out loud as He watched Peter run down the road to find a fishing pole.

God gave human beings the ability to create and enjoy humor. I think He gave us this ability because He knows that in this serious world we need to release an endorphin or two to relieve us of the stress of everyday life. In fact, laughing is one of the best medicines to get us out of whatever funk we find ourselves in each day.

As you go about your daily routine, why not find or create a reason to laugh? Do something that will cause someone else to laugh.

Dear Jesus, thank You for laughter. Please bring some laughter into my life today. And please help me to think of a way to bring laughter into someone else's life today. Amen.

IT IS WHAT IT IS

"If you do what is right, will you not be accepted? But if you do not do what is right, sin is crouching at your door; it desires to have you, but you must master it."
Genesis 4:7.

I love the staff members at my school. Each one of them has a unique package of gifts that they add to the fray of activity that often makes me break out in a huge grin.

Kyle Pepple, our math teacher, is no exception to this rule. Kyle grew up in a good-sized family with a dad who has coached basketball for Mercer Island High School forever. In fact, Kyle's father has coached and won more basketball games than any other person in the state of Washington. And Kyle got some of those coaching genes. Well, at least he got the voice of a coach.

At any given time during a school day, you can hear Kyle's voice ringing down the hall or in the office by the library or in the cafeteria. And the phrase I hear him proclaiming more than any other is "It is what it is. Deal with it."

If students find themselves in a quandary about grades or a relationship, or if Kyle's group is in charge of lunch and they run out of food, he looks at the situation, shrugs his shoulders, and says, "Hey, it is what it is. Deal with it."

I love that. It's total reality. *It is what it is. Deal with it.* And I think that in most cases that's a healthy way to look at whatever happens in life. View your situation for what it is, and make a decision on what you are going to do about it. Then act on your decision. Simple, right?

It's a good philosophy. The problem is that a lot of people on this earth find themselves in a situation and say, "It is what it is," and then they *don't* deal with it. Life hands them a bunch of lemons and they don't make lemonade, they just pout about the lemons until the lemons get rotten and stink up their life even more.

Peter was a pragmatist. He knew where he stood in the world, and he was fine with it. He was a C student at best. An average guy with an average life. He didn't get accepted into college, so he decided to follow in his dad's footsteps and become a fisherman. And Peter was probably an average-to-below-average fisherman. I say this because every time we find him fishing in the Bible, he had fished all night and had caught nothing . . . until Jesus said, "Throw your net on the other side of the boat."

Peter's life is a great example of "It is what it is. Deal with it."

As Jesus started to wind up His ministry on earth, Peter got a huge dose of "it is what it is, deal with it." Jesus celebrated Passover with His friends. The mood was somber. In fact, Peter noticed that Jesus was almost sad. It seemed that the whole world was weighing on His shoulders. They finished the "last supper" they would share with Jesus on this earth.

"When they had sung a hymn, they went out to the Mount of Olives. Then Jesus told them, 'This very night you will all fall away on account of me, for it is written: "I will strike the shepherd, and the sheep of the flock will be scattered." But after I have risen, I will go ahead of you into Galilee.' *Peter replied, 'Even if all fall away on account of you, I never will.' 'I tell you the truth,' Jesus answered, 'this very night, before the rooster crows, you will disown me three times.' But Peter declared, 'Even if I have to die with you, I will never disown you.' And all the other disciples said the same"* (Matthew 26:30-35).

Wow. How would you like to be in a class and have your teacher tell you ahead of time that no matter how hard you prepare, you are going to get an F on your test?

I mean, Jesus basically looked at Peter and said, "Hey, Peter, it is what it is. Deal with it."

Later on, as Jesus was on trial, Peter had his chance to experience "it is what it is." He denied that he even knew Jesus, just as His Master had predicted, and then he heard the rooster crow.

Peter had two roads to go down. He could deal with it the way Judas dealt with it, or he could take his lemons and make lemonade. Jesus gave him his chance in John 21, and Peter took the high road. He decided to stop wallowing in his failure and make choices that would eventually take him on the greatest adventure of his life.

It was what it was, and Peter dealt with it.

Every single one of us is living a life that is what it is. The question is How are we going to deal with it?

Are we going to wallow in our failures or learn from them and strive to be successful? Are we going to let a bad set of circumstances pull us down into a sour mood and a downcast heart, or are we going to grab the Savior's hand, get up, brush ourselves off, and go on with life?

Yes, life is what it is. Good and bad, it is what it is. There are some things about your life that you can't change. The past is the past. But (and I'm putting this as gently as I can) DEAL WITH IT!

Don't let your past steal your future. Don't let anything steal the possibilities that God has planned for you and your life. It is what it is. Now, you have some choices. Make great ones.

Dear Father, give me the courage to step out of a bad situation and walk hand in hand with You into a positive, forward-looking life. Amen.

WHAT ARE THE ODDS?

"I write these things to you who believe in the name of the Son of God so that you may know that you have eternal life."
1 John 5:13.

In the ridiculous comedy *Dumb and Dumber* a character named Lloyd Christmas looks deeply into the eyes of Mary Swenson (the girl he's been trying to find throughout the movie) and with a chip-toothed nervous grin blurts out his feelings, "What are the odds of a boy like you and a girl like me (yes, he got his genders mixed up) ending up together?"

A little surprised and confused, Mary looks at him and says honestly, "About one in a million."

Lloyd breaks out into an optimistic grin and says, "So you're sayin' there's a chance!"

I love long shots. When a long shot beats the odds, it's almost always a rewarding experience. When I was 18 years old, my sister, dad, and I traveled to Pasadena, California, to visit Aunt Fanny. Yes, that was her name. Aunt Fanny was a New Yorker who moved out West to live and help take care of my grandmother. She was about four feet ten and wrinkled like a prune that had soaked in the bathtub too long. And in the middle of her super-wrinkled face was a blotch of shiny bright-red lipstick. (I'm assuming that's where her lips were.) Aunt Fanny was little and wrinkled, but she could command attention with her wit and her famous New York accent. Oh, and Aunt Fanny loved to go to the racetrack and bet on horses.

On our visit, she insisted that we take her to San Anita, the horse track in the Los Angeles area. We did on the condition that my dad laid down, "Fanny, you can't bet any money at the racetrack. You are on a fixed income, and you aren't allowed to gamble it away."

"OK, Bobby, don't worry. I just like to watch the horses race," Fanny lied.

So we took Aunt Fanny to the track, and, of course, every time my dad turned around she was slipping money into my hands, whispering commands on which horses I was to lay bets on.

Aunt Fanny was having horrible luck with her money until the last race of the day. My dad wandered away from where we were sitting, and Aunt Fanny slipped some money into my hand. "Bet it all on Dr. W," she commanded!

I looked at my program. Dr. W was a long shot at 60-to-1 odds. I started to argue with her, but she stood at her full height, looked at me with her beady little eyes, and said, "I've got a feeling about this one—now get to it before I cause you some pain." She was serious, so I went and made the bet. Of course she won more than $1,500 when Dr. W galloped across the finish line in first place.

Everybody loves to watch the long shot come in first.

I can't tell you how many Christians I've met who feel like heaven is a long shot for them. Their question of God is "What are the chances of a God like You saving a guy like me?"

A lot of Christians feel like God's ultimate answer is "About one in a million."

Nothing could be further from God's intentions for you. At least that's not what the Bible teaches. Read this passage from 1 John 5:11-13:

"And this is the testimony: God *has given* us eternal life, and this life is in his Son. *He who has the Son has life*; he who does not have the Son of God does not have life. I write these things to you who believe in the name of the Son of God so *that you may know that you have eternal life*."

According to Scripture, being saved isn't some sort of guessing game. It's not a shot in the dark. In fact, it's just the opposite of that. It's a sure thing. The game is rigged in your favor. The Bible teaches us that God is deeply in love with you, and He went to the wildest extreme (His Son died on a cross) just to save you. If your response to that gift is to follow Him (as feeble as you feel your following is), then you are in—you get eternal life. It's not a million to one. It's not a thousand to one. It's not a hundred to one. It's a sure thing. Follow Jesus, and the gift of heaven is yours. It's that simple.

Dear Jesus, thank You for saving me. Forgive me when I doubt Your ability to love and save me as You've promised. Help me to act as though I'm saved, so that I can tell others about the good news of salvation. Amen.

HULK HOGAN VERSUS A BABY IN A MANGER

"The Word became flesh and made his dwelling among us. We have seen his glory, the glory of the One and Only, who came from the Father, full of grace and truth."
John 1:14.

A s will His second coming, Jesus' first coming took humanity by surprise. One day Mary received a visit from a heavenly being, a being brighter than the sun. He announced to her the inconceivable, the improbable, but by the same token, the inevitable and the planned. Mary had in her womb both the King of the universe and the Son of man . . . growing and developing, readying for birth.

And then, during a dark night on earth the blood, sweat, and anguish of labor produced a son—a peculiar fusion of man and God. The Promised One had arrived, and He was lying in a manger.

How confused Satan must have been. The moment that Adam and Eve fell, Satan must have wondered, *How will God attempt to redeem His prized possession? How will God save the apple of His eye, those whom He deeply loves? How will He do it?*

Of all the plans that the Godhead could have come up with to redeem humanity, isn't it a wonder that the infinite wisdom of God chose this course of action to save the world—the birth of a baby to bring an end to the great controversy and once again restore peace to the universe?

Christianity hinges on this claim, that Jesus was born of a virgin and that His Father was none other than God Himself. But what does it mean? Why is the incarnation of God so pivotal to Christianity? What did the Incarnation accomplish that couldn't have been done any other way? I'm sure that there are several reasons God chose to act as He did, but I'd like to share one that I think ranks toward the top.

I think one of the main reasons God chose to reveal Himself to humanity as a babe in a manger is mentioned in Philippians 2. It says this:

"Do nothing from selfish ambition or conceit, but in humility regard others as better than yourselves. Let each of you look not to your own interests, but to the interests of others. Let the same mind be in you that was in Christ

Jesus, who, though he was in the form of God, did not regard equality with God as something to be exploited, but emptied himself, taking the form of a slave, being born in human likeness. And being found in human form, he humbled himself and became obedient to the point of death—even death on a cross" (verses 3-8, NRSV).

Jesus came to earth the first time as an infant to show us how to live. The one lesson He tried to teach His disciples more than any other was that the last shall be first and the first shall be last. He even told parables about arrogant rich people meeting their doom and poor oppressed people receiving their overdue reward.

What a different world it would be if we could instill this idea into young people—the idea of a submissive spirit. But the world has other plans. It's now common for college and professional athletes, those whom we watch and at times idolize, to glory in the failures of their foes by some extraordinary display of humiliation. I call it the "I'm number one" syndrome.

The other night I was at home with a cold, and I was channel-surfing. As I was changing the channels, I happened on a professional wrestling program. I sat and watched these overgrown slabs of meat scream at each other until I was laughing.

It's shameful what we glory in nowadays, isn't it? The airwaves are teaching us how to be opposite of what Jesus tried to teach us as a babe in the manger. We watch this stuff, and we wonder why it is that the level of respect and regard for others is plummeting in our schools and in our homes.

The world teaches us to scream, "I'm number one!" while the still small voice of Christ tries to teach us the opposite of that. That baby, born in a manger, grew up and set an example for us in conduct and in attitude. And the above letter from Paul admonishes us to empty ourselves and have an attitude of submission toward one another.

Jesus, thank You for being born in a manger and giving us an example of humility and submission in our lives. Help me to tune out the selfishness of this world and focus on Your nature. Amen.

WEEDS ON THE WINDSHIELD

"He answered, 'I heard you in the garden,
and I was afraid because I was naked; so I hid.'"
Genesis 3:10.

Growing up, I was always big. Because of this, I was the same size as other children four years older than I was. And, consequently, as a youngster that's who I ended up hanging around too much of the time. I wanted to fit in, so sometimes I would do things that I thought the older kids would think was funny to gain their approval.

One summer night a group of older children and I were at a friend's house listening to music and playing games when someone suggested we walk up the very long hill to the Hilltop Grocery Store and get some goodies and soda pop. It was about 9:00 p.m. (where were our parents?) and dark out, but the road had wide sidewalks and pretty good lighting.

On our walk up the road the older kids started to tease me and give me a hard time. I'm sure it was harmless banter, but I felt like I needed to do something to turn the tide of teasing into a tidal wave of praise. So on our way back down the long hill, I found a big weed on the side of the road, uprooted it, and waited for an opportunity to impress.

It wasn't long before I got that opportunity. A beautiful 1968 Camero R/S was screaming down the hill and about to pass us when I tossed the clump of weeds (still attached to a lot of dirt and small rocks) up at the windshield of the speeding car. It was a direct hit.

The car immediately screeched its brakes and came to a sliding halt as five angry college-age students leaped out with the intention of breaking some heads. They were yelling and swearing as they ran toward our group. All my friends scattered and started running. I ran straight into the field of tall grass I had picked my weed grenade from and flopped on the ground, hoping that the tall grass would save my life.

The angry men were jumping all over the field looking for someone to punish for their cracked windshield. My heart was pounding in my throat. I was sure that one of my enemies was going to hear me breathing, find me hiding in the field, and throttle me for being a naughty boy. I was positive that I was going to die for my transgression. At one point, one of them stood two feet away from me, fuming out loud to a friend about the different ways he was going to punish the fiend who threw the missile at his car.

He finally stepped away. Shortly after that they gave up and drove off in a fury. My life was spared, and my older friends made even more fun of me than before.

I think I felt a little of what Adam and Eve must have felt in the garden, hiding in a grove, trying not to be found, trying to hide from what they felt would be the end of their lives. After all, they were told, "On the day you eat it, you will die."

What they didn't seem to know was that Jesus isn't an angry college student looking for revenge. He's a loving parent, a correcting, grace-filled friend who wanted to save Adam and Eve, not tear them limb from limb. And that's how He feels about you. You may throw a weed into God's windshield, either accidentally or in a fit of open defiance, but if you have found yourself in rebellion, thumbing your nose at God, you don't need to hide in the weeds. The Bible tells us that because of Jesus' sacrifice we can "approach the throne of grace with confidence, so that we may receive mercy and find grace to help us in our time of need" (Hebrews 4:16).

This tells me that when I do things contrary to God's will and get busted, I have only one direction to run. Not toward the weeds, but into the arms of a loving Father who is waiting to restore His child into the kind of person He's called him to be.

Dear God in heaven, forgive me when I'm defiant. Thank You for Your gift of forgiveness. Sometimes I really need it. Thank You for Your mercy. I couldn't live without it. Help me not to feel the need to impress the people around me. Help me to be secure in how You feel about me instead. Amen.

STARBUCKS GONE BAD

"I am not saying this because I am in need,
for I have learned to be content whatever the circumstances."
Philippians 4:11.

A few years ago my wife and I had an accident that left one of our cars in critical condition for about a month. So every morning I had to take a 45-minute bus ride into downtown Seattle, transfer to another bus, and ride it to the university I was attending.

Every once in a while my bus would arrive a little early or a little late, and I would have to stand at the bus stop downtown during rush hour, and wait. The place where I waited was literally in the middle of a bunch of skyscrapers in a section of town where scads of corporate types in expensive suits bustled by, talking on their cell phones, oblivious to the people around them.

One day, as I was waiting for my bus, I saw one of the most interesting paradoxes I've ever witnessed. Sitting against the wall a few feet away from me was a middle-aged homeless woman. It looked to me like she had not been able to change or wash her clothes in months. Every once in a while she would look up and ask whoever was walking by for some change. She chose a good place to sit, because just a few feet away was a Starbucks coffee stand. It was one of those portable ones on wheels that move around like a New York City hot dog stand. As people would get their change they'd drop a few coins into the little cup this woman was holding out.

As I was watching, a tall, very well dressed professional-looking woman walked by me. She approached the coffee vendor and purchased an extra-large cup of espresso. Then she turned and nearly tripped over the homeless woman's outstretched hand. Her sudden stop caused a small amount of coffee to slosh out of her cup and land on her blazer. It was then that the scene became interesting.

She looked down at this filthy, dirty homeless woman and started screaming at her. "Who's going to pay to get my jacket cleaned? Do you know how much this jacket cost? What if this stain doesn't come out? Can you pay for a new jacket?"

With that, she tossed the nearly full cup into an adjacent trash can and stomped off, leaving this homeless woman pretty stunned.

What was this woman's problem? Why would she get so upset with the situation that she found herself in? I would like to suggest that the reason she could stand in a $500 business suit and yell at a homeless person who was wearing all of the clothes she owned was that this woman had a huge deficiency in her ability to be thankful.

Being thankless has been one of the most serious problems in human history. Yet having a thankful heart is one of the most-talked-about traits of a good character that there is in the Bible.

In fact, there are 213 places in the Bible where it talks about God's people being thankful or needing to give thanks. And in the midst of all this thanksgiving talk in the Bible, we find ourselves, from time to time, like this woman, pouting about something that goes wrong in our life when, in some instance, we don't get our way.

There are very few things in this life that are more disgusting to look at than the actions of a thankless person.

When Jesus was on earth, He saw thankless people all the time. And I think it bothered Him. The book of Luke records a story that is just amazing. It says:

"As he entered a village, ten *lepers* approached him. Keeping their distance, they called out, saying, 'Jesus, Master, have mercy on us!' When he saw them, he said to them, 'Go and show yourselves to the priests.' And as they went, they were made clean. Then one of them, when he saw that he was healed, turned back, praising God with a loud voice. He prostrated himself at Jesus' feet and thanked him. And he was a Samaritan. Then Jesus asked, 'Were not ten made clean? But the other nine, where are they? Was none of them found to return and give praise to God except this foreigner?' Then he said to him, 'Get up and go on your way; your faith has made you well'" (Luke 17:12-19, NRSV).

Jesus was bothered by the fact that only one out of the 10 people He healed was thankful enough to come back and say thank you.

How many times in our lives have we been like the "other nine"? God blesses us in thousands of ways, and yet we find ourselves living our lives as though somebody just stained our blazer with a little coffee. We pout because things don't go as we plan. Or we get all bent out of shape because somebody else's stupidity put a wrinkle in our schedule. I sincerely believe that all of this kind of behavior has its roots in not being a truly thankful person.

And being a thankless person flies directly in the face of what Scripture admonishes us to be. Paul expressed his desire to be thankful and for us to be thankful people. Listen to what he says in three different texts:

"Of course, there is great gain in godliness combined with contentment; for we brought nothing into the world, so that we can take nothing out of it; but if we have food and clothing, we will be content with these" (1 Timothy 6:6-8, NRSV).

"Not that I am referring to being in need; for I have learned to be content with whatever I have" (Philippians 4:11, NRSV).

"Keep your lives free from the love of money, and be content with what you have; for he has said, 'I will never leave you or forsake you'" (Hebrews 13:5, NRSV).

Being content is the biggest result of being a thankful person. And there is no better feeling in the world than the feeling of being content with what you have.

But being thankful has become foreign to us in a society that never seems to be satisfied. The world tells us that we need to have the latest car, the newest fashion, and see the latest hit movie. And when we are done getting and doing all of the latest stuff, are we thankful? No way. As soon as we get the latest whatever, the guy next to us gets a newer one, and we start all over again, never being thankful for the blessings we have.

Now, all of us get trapped in being thankless from time to time, but how can you tell if you've become like the woman in the expensive suit? How can you tell if you've truly become a thankless person?

Take some time today in prayer and ask God if there are things in your life that are barriers to a thankful, contented life. Another suggestion is to spend some time on a regular basis in service to those who are less fortunate than you. And finally, look through your house at all your stuff. Take an inventory of all the things you need versus what you don't need. Could you live on less and give more?

God, please teach me to be content in all circumstances. Amen.

WHAT DO YOU WANT?

"I am not ashamed of the gospel, because it is the power of God for the salvation of everyone who believes: first for the Jew, then for the Gentile."
Romans 1:16.

There used to be an amusing commercial on television for an ice-cream bar. The question was asked, "What would you do for a Klondike bar?" The commercial would ask people what strange and embarrassing things they would do for a Klondike bar. In fact, people still go to ridiculous lengths to get a bite of a Klondike bar.

When I was chaplain at Mount Pisgah Academy in North Carolina, once a year I would have a day dedicated to seeing what lengths a group of students would go to get something as ridiculous and silly as an ice-cream bar.

It would go like this: I would split the kids into about six groups of 10. They would have to go to several stations and try crazy things to impress staff members who acted as judges. The team that achieved the highest scores would end up winning the contest.

One station had the kids trying to get from point A to point B with the fewest feet touching the ground. Another station asked the students to bob for cherry tomatoes in a big vat of tapioca pudding. Yuck! The prize for the winning team? A Klondike bar, of course.

Obviously a Klondike bar was pretty good motivation for a group of teenagers to do some pretty brave (and disgusting) things.

What do you want? What are you willing to do to get it?

As I read the New Testament and history of the early church, I'm continually amazed at what the apostles and early fathers and mothers of our church went through to achieve their calling in Christ. Many of them experienced incredible persecution—sitting in jail for years, beatings, and abandonment from family and friends are some of the smaller problems they had to go through. At one point the apostle Paul felt compelled to write the words below:

"We are hard pressed on every side, but not crushed; perplexed, but not in despair; persecuted, but not abandoned; struck down, but not destroyed.

We always carry around in our body the death of Jesus, so that the life of Jesus may also be revealed in our body" (2 Corinthians 4:8-10).

Wow! What commitment, what determination, what dedication. They wanted to serve their God much more than any human being has ever wanted a Klondike bar.

How is it that people would do almost anything for a Klondike bar, but sharing the gospel with a neighbor, being inconvenienced on a mission trip, or simply bowing their head for a short prayer of thanks before a meal in public is just too much to handle? People seem to wilt in the face of any pressure or possible embarrassment.

What do you want? What are you willing to do to get it? My answer? I want to honor God and be open to His calling in my life. What am I willing to do to get it? Well, I guess that remains to be seen.

Jesus, give me the deep desire to do anything that You call me to do. Help me to be bold in my faith. Help me to gladly serve You, even when it's uncomfortable.
Amen.

SATAN'S IN MY HEAD

"For when we were controlled by the sinful nature, the sinful passions aroused by the law were at work in our bodies, so that we bore fruit for death."

Romans 7:5.

One of the joys of working with elementary-aged students is listening to the things that come out of their mouths and trying not to laugh while they are saying them.

My wife once had a kindergartner announce to her class that they were "half Mexican and half vegetarian." On another occasion while talking with her class about appropriate and inappropriate language and gestures, with wide-eyed vivid description she had a student say, "My mom doesn't have a potty mouth, but my daddy likes to swear at the other drivers on the road. He also sticks his middle finger up at them. I don't know what that means, but I know that it's not good."

The fourth-grade teacher announces to her parents that if they won't believe half of what their children say about her, she won't believe half of what their kids say about them.

Just today, as I was sitting in my office, I heard another doozie that made me snicker and then ponder the import that can come only from the mouth of babes.

Little Maddie is in first grade and is rarely if ever in trouble. She's one of those kids who just looks like a little grown-up. Short for her age, she carries herself like a self-confident leader and has been heard directing traffic on the playground better than a seasoned teacher's aide.

Today Maddie was sent to the office for being too wiggly and not sitting still. My office manager happens to be Maddie's aunt. It was their conversation that I overheard.

"Maddie, why did you get sent to the office?" asked Auntie Tammy.

"'Cause I couldn't sit still. I keep getting out of my seat and wandering around," responded Maddie.

As she was standing in front of her aunt, Maddie was wiggling and moving her feet. "Do you have to go to the bathroom?" Tammy asked.

"Nope."

"Well, then, what's the matter?" asked Tammy.

"I don't really know. I think Satan's in my head," confessed the first grader.

It was all Tammy could do not to break out in loud guffaws. She explained that having the wiggles in class isn't Satan living in her head—it's just a part of being 6 years old. Maddie did her time in the office and then went back to her class and had a more settled rest of the day.

Satan's in my head. In the 1970s there was a comedian named Flip Wilson who coined the saying "The devil made me do it."

I think that the devil is responsible for a lot of the woes in this world, but I'm wondering if he couldn't just take a vacation and we'd carry on his work fine without his help.

I once saw a bumper sticker that said, "Lead us not into temptation, *I can find it all by myself.*"

The Bible describes us as being made up of two natures, a spiritual one and a sinful one. That explains the war that goes on in our heads when we are tempted to do or be something opposite of God's calling in our lives.

You would think it would be a naturally easy choice. Always choose the good, loving, pure, true, gentle way, right? Well, as we all know, it's not that simple. There is a war going on inside of us that is calling for our loyalty. And in a weird sense, the devil is in our heads. But he's not alone. God's Spirit is also living in us, wooing us into the kind of relationship with our Creator that would lead us to say no to the devil in our heads and yes to the promptings of His Holy Spirit.

Dear Father, please help me to be tuned in to Your voice. Help me to be able to identify the voice of this world and then ignore it as I attempt to listen to and then do Your perfect will. Amen.

YOU'RE NO ONE IN MY BOOK

"Again, if the trumpet does not sound a clear call, who will get ready for battle?"
1 Corinthians 14:8.

I was sitting in my office today, and I received the most confusing text message I've ever received. It was from Sharon Searson, one of my conference educational superintendents. The text said, "You are no one in my book."

I was shocked. I was taken aback. I was a little hurt. I was hurt because Sharon is one of my favorite people in the whole world. And for some reason Sharon has always communicated to me that she thought I could walk on water. When she went through difficult times in life, she called me for pastoral advice and care. When I would preach for conference education weekends, Sharon would be on the front row laughing and crying to the same sermon she had heard five times before. And afterward she would always say, "You are my favorite preacher. I could listen to you every week."

When considering a move back into church ministry, Sharon once told me, "I would switch churches if you got a church in the area that wasn't the one we attend now."

I love Sharon Searson. Everyone needs a Sharon Searson to warp their sense of self-worth and make them feel better about themselves.

And here I sat, staring at a text message from my biggest fan, "You are no one in my book." Ouch. What did I do? What had I said to offend her?

Three minutes later my phone dinged again. Another text message. This one again from Sharon. "You are number one in my book." And then the phone call.

In a panic, Sharon explained that she was sitting in a workshop in which the instructor had asked each person with a cell phone to send an encouraging text message to someone they admired. She wasn't an experienced texter, but she managed to send off the first message. Then, after sending it, she read it again, and to her horror, she discovered that a period after the "no" would have better communicated her feelings. She quickly followed with the second text and the phone call to clarify her first text. And we both had a great laugh because of it.

Boy, it's easy to be misunderstood, isn't it? How many times have we tried our best to communicate an idea or an emotion only to have it fall on ears that misinterpreted or misunderstood our intended meaning?

From the beginning of Creation, God has tried to give human beings a clear picture of who He is. Through patriarchs, prophets, and kings, God called His people to know Him as the person He is. And in just the right time, His plan came to fruition through His Son, Jesus Christ.

Jesus came to earth as a direct communication from the Father. God wanted to clear up the confusion as to who He is and how people view Him. John 14:9 says: "Anyone who has seen me [Jesus] has seen the Father." Nothing confusing about that. When we look at Jesus, we see God the Father in all His glory, in all His mercy, and in all His love. This message from heaven is crystal clear. No need to send another message. God loves me so much that He sent His Son to die for me so that I might live with Him forever.

Dear Jesus, thank You for the clear message of the Father's love. Thanks for living and dying to show me the Father and how He feels about me. Amen.